BY TYSON COLE
AND JESSICA DUPUY

FOREWORD BY
LANCE ARMSTRONG

# uchi

## THE COOKBOOK

**PHOTO CREDITS**

Paul Bardagjy: Pages ii-iii, 9

Kenny Braun: Page 4

Brett Buchanan: Page 265
  (Courtesy *Austin Business Journal*)

Tyson Cole: Pages 22-23, 38, 82-83, 152-153, 162,
  188-189

Jennifer Davick: Pages i, viii, 3, 12-13, 17, 36-37,
  40-41, 52-53

Rebecca Fondren: Pages 50-51, 54-55, 58-81, 89-91,
  94-96, 101-103, 106-108, 111, 115, 119-121, 124-126,
  128-129, 132-133, 142-143, 146-148, 151, 154, 156-157,
  160-161, 164-165, 167-169, 176, 179-181, 184-186,
  191-193, 196, 199, 202-203, 206-208, 215, 217-219,
  222-223, 226-228, 233-235, 236, 238-239, 242-243,
  245-247, 250-251

Randal Ford: Cover, Page 43

Jennifer Hellow: Pages 6-7, 35, 39, 44, 48-49, 56-57,
  87, 98-99, 112, 116-117, 134-135, 170-171, 194-195,
  200-201, 210-211, 224, 230-231, 252-253, 256-257,
  262-263

Mark Miks: Pages 14-15, 18, 19, 24-25, 48

George Schemagin: Pages 32-33, 266-267

Philip Speer: Pages 28-29

**UMASO PUBLISHING**

701 South Lamar, Suite C, Austin, Texas 78704

Copyright © 2011 Tyson Cole
Copyright © 2011 Jessica Dupuy
Copyright © 2011 Lance Armstrong
Copyright © 2011 Rebecca Fondren
Copyright © 2011 Jennifer Davick
Copyright © 2011 Jennifer Hellow

Library of Congress Control Number: 2010940462

Distributed through University of Texas Press
P.O. Box 7819, Austin, Texas 78713-7819
800-252-3206  www.utexaspress.com

Book and jacket design by
DJ Stout and Julie Savasky
Pentagram Design, Austin, Texas

Happy Birthday
Gretchen!

*Uchi, The Cookbook* has been a project in the works for a long time. We've spent the past eight years at Uchi taking the aesthetic of Japanese cuisine and making it better, with little tweaks on flavors, textures, and ingredients. I love getting to watch people experience our food for the first time. And I love watching them come back time and time again for more. For me, creating Uchi has been the best venue to display my love for this style of food and to be a gracious host to those who trust us to give them an unforgettable experience. It's like welcoming people into my own home.

This restaurant, and therefore this book, would not have been possible without those who have played an integral part in this entire story. I would especially like to thank:

Daryl Kunik, for being one of my sushi customers from the very beginning and for believing enough in what I do to make it into a successful restaurant. Thank you for your hard work and for taking the chance.

Paul Qui, for your extraordinary talent and vision in pushing me and Uchi cuisine to the next level.

Philip Speer, for your amazing hard work

and diligent organization. You keep it all together for us. Your impeccable cooking skills not only as a pastry chef but with the entire Uchi menu are invaluable. Thank you in particular for piecing together all of our recipes for this book.

Jessica Dupuy, for your time, talent, and dedication in helping me put this book together and bring it to reality.

Mostly, my wife, Rebekkah, for your love and endless support of the time and dedication it's taken me to make Uchi into what it is today. I love you.

And, to our three newest additions: Aubrie (6), Larkin (3), and Amelia (9 months) Cole.

Other key people have played a part not only in this book but in helping me get where I am today:

Masa Saio, Vu Le, Yoshi Okai, Justin Sells, Deegan McClung, Mat Clouser, Kaz Edwards, Ted Kasuga, Kiyohisa Hara, Motoyasu Utsunomiya, Takehiko Fuse, DJ Stout and Julie Savasky of Pentagram Design, Dana Frank, Samantha Davidson, and UT Press.

TYSON COLE

# CONTENTS

# RECIPES

# SUSHI, IN AUSTIN?

A LOT CAN HAPPEN IN 20 YEARS. IN THE EARLY 90S, I DIDN'T TOUCH THE STUFF, AND NOT MANY IN THIS TOWN DID. LIKE MOST TRANS- PLANTS TO AUSTIN, ONCE I GOT HERE, I BURROWED MY ROOTS INTO THE LIMESTONE AND "GOT LOCAL." IT WAS EASY TO GET LOCAL THEN. THE TOWN WAS SMALL, PARKING AT WHOLE FOODS WAS QUICK, AND YOU COULD WEAR JEANS TO THE BEST RESTAURANT IN TOWN.

I was living in Como, Italy, during the racing season and had just become the youngest world champion in cycling history. My buddy Tyson Cole was washing dishes on Congress Avenue in one of the few sushi restaurants in town.

Every year, I live in Europe during the racing season and return to Austin in the off-season. Leaving each time gives me a unique view of this town, because I get to come home to see what has changed. Over the past two decades, Austin has grown up while Tyson has honed his skills with a sharp knife. And both have managed to do it well—really well. We all reminisce about the good old days, when the roads were less crowded and the rides more carefree, but the new and different is what really marks the passage of time and gives this place its magical energy today.

Uchi is a perfect example of that energy. Uchi is the best sushi restaurant in the world— bar none. I say it. I believe it. I'm willing to prove it to anyone who doubts it. When I tell visiting friends from all over the world that we're going to Uchi, they often twist up their faces and say, "Sushi, in Austin?"

And then Tyson serves up his signature cuisine and shuts them up every time.

This is a guy who obsesses about quality, with a drive and a special ingenuity that consistently deliver magic to the table every night. These are clean, fresh, surprising dishes, not variations of old standards or "me too" approaches to food. Each time I walk out of Uchi, I'm certain I've received the very best from the most talented chef I know. And he never fails to blow the minds of friends and acquaintances who may have underestimated just how good sushi can be in this city.

Now this former dishwasher turned world-class chef has given us an Austin icon and raised the bar of expectation for what Austinites can proclaim and deliver to anyone from anywhere—the best damn dining experience they will ever have.

Plus, you can still wear jeans.

Enjoy this book. I know you will enjoy the food.

Well done, Tyson.

LANCE ARMSTRONG

# A TRANSFORMATIVE EXPERIENCE

SURE, THERE ARE PLENTY OF 5-STAR RESTAURANTS THAT DAZZLE WITH KID-GLOVED SERVICE AND AMBITIOUS MULTICOURSE MEALS. BUT UCHI STANDS ALONE IN ITS BRILLIANT SIMPLICITY AND ITS COZY CHARM. YOU MAY FIND A CHEF'S TASTING MENU HERE, BUT THIS PLACE LEAVES OUT ALL OF THE "POMP" AND ASKS YOU ONLY TO ARRIVE—WITH AN OPEN MIND—FOR THE UNFORGETTABLE "CIRCUMSTANCE."

We added this reflection pond at the entrance to Uchi when we redesigned the restaurant in 2003. I liked the idea of having a view of water from the sushi bar.

"Uchi" is Japanese for "house," and as the name implies, this nationally acclaimed restaurant is in a modest 1920s bungalow. On any given evening, you may have to wait up to two hours for a table. But whether you're waiting with a cocktail in the Japanese garden patio or just taking your seat in the welcoming dining room, you can't help but feel you're witnessing a special performance.

While there really is no bad seat in the house, a spot at the sushi bar allows you into the very heart of the restaurant. When you first take your seat, a friendly server greets you with a steaming hand towel and a comprehensive list of sake and wine. As your towel is whisked away, another server welcomes you with a bite-size gift from the kitchen, a small preview of the evening designed to excite every taste bud. Something like a bright square of compressed watermelon, a dash of homemade fish sauce, and a sprinkle of Maldon salt—a perplexing combination to be sure, but one that tastes like heaven.

The best advice for dining here: Let the servers make selections for you. They will lead you to a jackpot of the day's most recent arrivals. Trust them with your first order while you take a moment to look over the menu. Yes, you could order a spicy tuna or rainbow roll, but

that would be missing the point of Uchi. In this whimsical house of creativity where Japanese tradition meets a kaleidoscope of unexpected flavors, it's best to choose discerningly among the more playful dishes on the menu. Why settle for safe and ordinary when the beauty of Uchi is its flair for the provocative and unexpected? This is, after all, more of a journey than it is a meal.

Particularly if you try the simple yet distinct flavors of the maguro tuna, coupled with slices of crisp Fuji apple, goat cheese, cracked pepper, and pumpkin seed oil, altogether a momentous explosion of separate but familiar flavors fused into a holy union. Or a simple sea bream sashimi, sliced thin like a frosty pane of glass, atop a bright sprig of Japanese mint and a warm lump of sushi rice, sprinkled with fragrant lemon zest and drizzled with olive oil. Each dish is a celebration of texture and flavor, one that proclaims a simple truth: To eat at Uchi is to taste in high definition.

The first time you dine here, you'll notice there's something about the setting that is hip yet disarming. The warm and inviting den features red-papered walls dappled with cherry blossom sketches, low-lit basket chandeliers dangling from the ceiling like glowing beehives, and an

open arrangement of cozy but not cramped dining room seating. The ambient music, always a low-tempo beat, blends with the steady stream of patrons arriving through the front door to snag a spot on the growing wait list.

Behind the bar stands a sentry of sushi chefs dressed in white and armed with well-worn cutting boards and expertly sharpened single-edged Japanese knives. They stand for hours, hands reaching for fresh fish, oils, special sauces, garnishes, and warm plates from the window of the perpetually buzzing kitchen behind them. Their knives are like silver phantoms rapidly slicing and paring small cuts of fish, fruits, and vegetables. Each cut is clean. Each cut is precise. Each cut creates quite possibly the most perfect bite you've ever experienced.

Delivering that perfect bite is the one mission of executive chef and owner Tyson Cole. In contrast to the predominantly Asian makeup of the sushi chefs behind the counter, their slight, unassuming fair-skinned boss is himself a Florida native raised in Texas. Though he is fluent in the language, he has spent only a mere couple of weeks on Japanese soil. Yet Cole has managed to create a Japanese restaurant that has caught the eye of the country's culinary critics ever since it opened in 2003, deep in the heart of Texas.

The sushi bar, with its seemingly endless supply of fresh fish—primarily from Tokyo's famed Tsukijo fish market—displays a rainbow of delightful selections adorned with fresh fruits and vegetables and a curious assortment of micro greens. Small cedar boxes line the top of the case, filled with everything from golden raisins and black sesame seeds to crisply fried wafers of fish scales and exotic sea salts.

But you needn't be at the sushi bar to enjoy the show. Uchi tantalizes your senses anywhere you're seated, with servers who deliver an infinite number of artful dishes in a manner calculated to elicit animated reactions from fellow diners. It's impossible not to glance at what creation just arrived at the table beside you. Is it the sweet and crisp melon gazpacho adorned with luscious morsels of poached lobster? Or the polenta custard, corn sorbet, and corn milk dessert—a blissful homage to summer corn?

As you savor your meal and as the feeling of having just experienced something unfor-gettable washes over you, look for a friendly character in a simple white chef's coat. He moves fluidly between his post at the kitchen counter, where he meticulously inspects each dish, and the dining room, where he warmly greets guests and often brings bites from the kitchen to surprised and grateful diners. It's his effortless way of converting even the most begrudging sushi skeptic into a fervent believer in the Uchi way of food. His genuine kindness, candor, and enthusiasm for his craft are what attract an ardent cadre of followers to this little cottage restaurant on the south side of Austin every night. After all, this is Tyson Cole's house, and you are very welcome.

When we opened Uchi, it was important to maintain a warm atmosphere. We used Asian influences overall, but we really want people to feel as if they have been a guest in our home.

# IF I COULD USE ONE WORD TO

## DESCRIBE MYSELF, IT WOULD BE "PERFECTIONIST." BUT NOT IN SOME UPPITY, POMPOUS INTERPRETATION OF THE TERM. IT'S MORE ABOUT THE WAY I APPROACH THINGS. EVEN AS A KID, GROWING UP NEAR SARASOTA AND LATER OUTSIDE HOUSTON, I WANTED THINGS TO BE PERFECT. WHETHER IT WAS HOW I BUILT MY LEGO SETS, ATE MY FOOD

I spent more than a decade moving through the many stages of becoming a sushi chef. Throughout that time I never imagined I'd one day own a restaurant. It's been a long journey, but it's taught me the importance of learning from the people around me and being the best host I can be for my customers.

by ensuring that my fork had all the components of a perfect bite, arranged my sock drawer, or organized my car—if something interested me, I focused on it completely. To me, it's always been about aesthetics and organization. If I could make something clean and simple but also beautiful and appealing, I was satisfied—well, almost.

I spent the first part of my career doing odd jobs—in roofing and construction, as a camp counselor in the Catskills, as a Little League umpire—but none of those clicked with this need to shape and perfect. It wasn't until my early twenties, when I was living in Austin, that I found sushi. I was between jobs and living with a girlfriend, hoping to transfer to The University of Texas but in reality spending my time like most twenty-somethings without a plan: drinking, smoking, and sleeping. I was lost. One morning, I woke up to my girlfriend standing over me. She said, "Tyson, if you don't get a job today, we're done, and you're out of here."

So I got up. I took a bus downtown to Congress Avenue and put in applications at every place I passed. After a week, the only place that called me back was Kyoto Japanese Restaurant to fill a dishwasher position. I took it. At first, I kind of hated it. I had never had sushi before and thought it was disgusting. But they would put food out at "family meal" every day, and

soon, I was addicted. That fresh hit of protein was just perfect. Eventually I started moving up from dishwasher to cook to waiter and then to sushi chef at the bottom of the line. It was really hard work, but my father was a Marine, so I was raised with that type of work ethic.

In time, I managed to earn the respect of the Japanese sushi chefs there. After work, I'd hang out with them at bars and at their apartments. I didn't speak a word of Japanese, but I slowly began to learn by watching Japanese game shows and food shows with them. That was the first time I saw *Iron Chef Japan*. I'll never forget the first time I saw a young Morimoto in a shiny silver uniform. I thought he was so awesome. Who knew that years later, I'd be facing him on *Iron Chef America*?

At that time, the best sushi restaurant in Austin was Musashino. I didn't have a car, so I had a friend drive me up there. It was beyond anything I'd seen. I had no idea sushi had such reach, the ability to be so striking and unique. The textures were incredible, the fish was pristine. At the sushi bar stood four Japanese sushi chefs, clad in traditional chef robes and bandannas. The sushi case had huge pieces of fish. (I was used to frozen precut sushi fish at Kyoto.) The chefs had beautiful Japanese knives and wooden cutting boards as opposed to the plastic ones I was used to. The chefs all

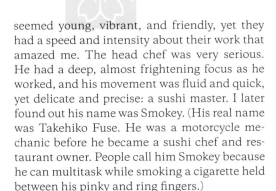

seemed young, vibrant, and friendly, yet they had a speed and intensity about their work that amazed me. The head chef was very serious. He had a deep, almost frightening focus as he worked, and his movement was fluid and quick, yet delicate and precise: a sushi master. I later found out his name was Smokey. (His real name was Takehiko Fuse. He was a motorcycle mechanic before he became a sushi chef and restaurant owner. People call him Smokey because he can multitask while smoking a cigarette held between his pinky and ring fingers.)

That first experience at Musashino changed my life. By then, I knew that being a sushi chef was for me. It was all I could think about. And I was determined to work for Smokey. I went back to Musashino a second night to meet him. I asked him what I needed to do to get a job with him, and he said, "Can you read and write Japanese?"

"No."

He replied, "You could never work here."

I was crushed. I had found exactly what I wanted to do in life but couldn't have it. It was agony.

About two weeks later, someone started banging on my bedroom window at 3 o'clock in the morning. I opened my curtain to see a guy I recognized from Musashino. He pointed to my front door to let him in. So I opened the door, and it was this crazy-looking Japanese guy and Smokey. They walked into my living room with a big bucket filled with ice and cans of Budweiser.

He offered me a beer and told me to sit down. After a few sips of his own beer, he said, "We want you to come work for us."

I said, "I *want* to work for you."

He told me he would double my pay from Kyoto and said, "You start Monday."

Then he grabbed a couple beers from his bucket, set them on the table, and left.

That was it. That was the job interview. I was sitting on my couch, in my underwear, with a Budweiser at 3 o'clock in the morning, and I had scored a job at Musashino. Apparently, the crazy Japanese guy who was banging on my window was friends with one of the chefs at Kyoto, who had told him about how hard I worked. I guess they decided to take a risk.

I went from the Little Leagues of sushi in Austin to the Big Leagues. I was like a dove in a

field of shotguns. I was scared shitless. But that was when I really started to learn Japanese. I was on the sushi line with chefs who didn't speak any English. I bought videotapes and books to learn the language. I was suddenly immersed in an entirely new and foreign culture, and I loved every second of it. Instantly, I had become part of a family with the other sushi chefs. I would hang out with them after work and pick up things. Still, it was hard to get up to speed on the culture and language while, at the same time, trying to work my way up the sushi line.

People always ask me how many times I've been to Japan. I've been there once. But I was in Japanese culture day in and day out for seven straight years. I was in it every day. At work. Before work. After work. That was it. It was like living in Japan in Austin.

At that time, I thought I would make sushi forever, maybe move to Japan and marry a Japanese woman. I was sold. The Japanese just have a level of respect for life in general. If they do something, it is 110 percent all the time. They say what they mean, and they mean what they say. And their work ethic is much the same.

One of the first fish that I learned to cut was mackerel. It's viewed as the "training" fish for sushi chefs because it's so cheap. If you mess up while breaking it down, it's not as big of a deal as with a nice piece of fish like toro. Once you get good at breaking down mackerel, you move on to more complicated fish.

As a sushi chef, you have to be quick. There are thousands of skills that you have to learn; most of it is just with a knife. More than anything, it's about dexterity. A tactile sense of what's around you at your workstation is important too. Your moves have to be precise, and you have to feel a balance within the space you're working. There were many Saturday nights at Musashino that went by like a blur. Sometimes I would step back and have to pinch myself. I couldn't believe how thrilling it all was. I'd be coordinating orders in Japanese with the sushi chefs, managing countless order tickets, talking with customers about their families and jobs, cooking eel in toaster ovens behind me, and waving around my razor-sharp knife, carving through endless pieces of fish. I was so hot, I'd be covered in sweat. It was choreographed chaos and the adrenaline high was invigorating. I couldn't wait to wake up each morning and do it all over again.

My advantage the whole time was that I was an English speaker, so I was great with customers. They really started trusting me and would let me make them whatever I wanted. Smokey saw how powerful that rapport with customers was for business, and it gave him more trust in me.

That's when he took me to Japan. He took me to meet his family and all around Tokyo to all sorts of sushi restaurants. He showed me how the Japanese live and work and eat every day. I was like a kid in a candy shop. I was entranced with everything I saw.

When we returned to Austin, I couldn't fight this feeling that I wanted something more. I had grown so much at Musashino, but I was still confined by Smokey's expectations. It was his restaurant, and he was adamant about serving traditional Japanese cuisine. I wanted to step out of that mold and take that to another level.

I actually took a job at Bond Street in New York, but it wasn't long before I realized that I really wanted to be in Austin. So I went back to Musashino, but I wasn't satisfied. Smokey could tell. He promised me one day he would give me the restaurant, but I would have to wait for him to retire. I didn't want to wait that long.

I had a customer who came in all the time to eat my sushi. He had followed me from my

**More than 20 percent of our sales at Uchi are sushi rolls, or makimono. Sushi rolls are the intro level for most people just learning to eat sushi, and it's really what most people associate with the cuisine. We have a two-person station devoted to making our makimono each night just to keep things moving at a good pace.**

days at Kyoto. His name was Daryl Kunik, and over time we became friends. He started talking to me about the idea of opening my own restaurant, and it didn't take long for me to believe it was a good idea. Smokey thought I was stupid for doing so. I'd like to think he was proud of me, but he's not the type to let you know that kind of thing. We drank sake at his house late one night, and he told me in Japanese that if I wanted to make him proud, I would have to open a restaurant that made sushi in the traditional Japanese way.

And I responded in Japanese, "No way, Smokey-san. I'm going to let you continue to do that at Musashino. I can't do that. I'm not Japanese. I'm going to take what you've taught me, and I'm going to make *my* kind of food."

## UCHI BEGINS

About a year later, Daryl and I had a location and investors, and we were ready to open the doors to our new restaurant. Daryl would be the business partner, and I would be the chef. It was in an old house in a part of town that, at the time, didn't have much going for it. The house was also the site of many failed restaurant concepts, but we were determined to make our sushi concept work.

I've always loved art and the aesthetics of different letters and typography. I was constantly writing down names for the restaurant I hoped to have. Late one night after work, I was writing down the name of a friend of mine from Musashino in Japanese. When I broke it up, the word "uchi" was there.

In 2002, we purchased Si Bon, a former French restaurant on South Lamar. This is a picture of me in front of the building before we started renovating it. I remember feeling so overwhelmed by all the little details that went into designing the restaurant. All I knew how to do was make sushi. Running a restaurant was a learn-as-you-go process from that point on.

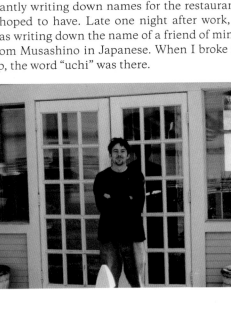

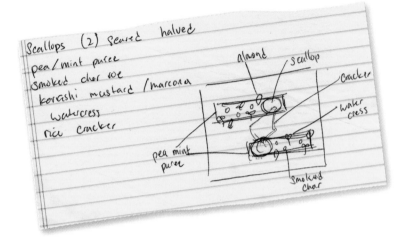

Scallops (2) seared halved
pea/mint puree
Smoked char roe
korashi mustard/marcona
watercress
rice cracker

almond — scallop
cracker
water cress
pea mint puree
smoked char

**Composed dishes at Uchi are all about creative ideas and specific planning. We sketch most of our dishes and include a list of all the components to include with them. Once we're happy with the complete dish, we use the sketches as road maps for the chefs at the stations in the kitchen where the dishes are prepared for the night.**

I really liked the way it looked. I loved how the letters were: curved-curved-curved-line. I also liked how it had two consonants in the middle and to vowels on the ends. I looked it up in Japanese and found that "uchi" means "house." It was perfect. We had just bought a house for the restaurant, and there was something very meaningful about being able to invite people into my home to eat my food.

We opened in May 2003. I was a mess. We had a motley crew for staff when we started. After six months, Dale Rice of the *Austin American-Statesman* reviewed us and gave us only two stars. I was crushed. But he was right on the things he railed me on. He talked about service, atmosphere, and a few food items. Everything he said was very constructive.

So we changed some things, and within a year or so, we were really hitting our stride. We started getting more local press, and then in 2005, I remember I was prepping one day and I got a phone call from someone with *Food & Wine* magazine. I went outside to take the call and it was Dana Cowin, the editor in chief of the magazine. She said, "I'm calling to tell you that you just won one of *Food & Wine*'s Top 10 Chefs in America."

I freaked out. I stood on one of the outside tables and screamed. It was such a validation for the work we had done. I know it was about the commitment to the food we were serving, and it was the real sign for me that we were going to make it.

That was the tipping point. We were managing one- to two-hour waits every night of the week. We were going through so much product, barely enough to keep up. I used to have to struggle to get my purveyors to provide what I needed, but all of a sudden they were giving us even better product from even more places. It became a catch-22: We would get so busy because the sushi was so fresh. Well, the sushi was so fresh because we were so damn busy that we were constantly bringing new product in.

As a chef and an owner, I had to learn how to manage my time, and I had to learn how to lead people, something I had never really done before. I was always more of a "lead by example" type of person, but I eventually had to learn how to delegate and take myself out of the picture. Coming off the sushi line was the hardest thing for me by far. That was my comfort zone. It's where I felt I had the most control. But my staff kicked me off the line. It was almost like an intervention.

I was very resistant to leaving, but it was one of the best things I could have done. So many chefs get caught up in staying in the spot with the most control, and it prevents them from being able to see the whole picture, from learning from the people working for them. Once I came off of my station, it was like all these clouds opened up, and I could really see the whole restaurant. I realized I could touch everything and interact with the customers everywhere. If you could quantify levels of maturity or growth for me at Uchi, that was the final level for me. All of a sudden, everything was clear. I had gone from being a dishwasher at a sushi restaurant to serving the best sushi in town at a restaurant of my very own.

# THE UCHI FOOD FORMULA IS SIMPLE:

WE GET THE VERY BEST INGREDIENTS AND COMBINE THEM IN NEW AND UNIQUE WAYS TO MAKE THEM EVEN BETTER. FOOD IS USUALLY BEST WHEN YOU KEEP IT SIMPLE. WE COMBINE INGREDIENTS FOR THAT "UMAMI" QUALITY, TO MAKE THINGS DELICIOUS—THAT "WOW" FACTOR. UCHI FOOD IS CRISP, LIGHT, REFRESHING, FEMININE, AND USER-FRIENDLY TO THE AMERICAN PALATE.

Uchi's head sushi chef is Masazumi Saio. He's been with us from the very beginning. I actually had to bring him over here from Japan on a student visa. He had no experience at the time, but I knew him through a friend and learned that he was a hard worker. Today he's one of the most valuable people at the restaurant.

But the Uchi experience goes beyond great food. For so long, it was about perfection for me. It wasn't until after Uchi came into play that I realized that my desire all along has been hospitality, to give. It's not just about skills, work ethic, and creativity. It's about the desire to make people happy. To me, that's just so fulfilling. I want people to see, feel, and taste what I love most about Japanese food. How clean it is. How light it is. How delicate it is, with its array of textures and flavors.

When I first started on a sushi line, I came to like having new people sit in front of me for their meal. I liked serving them dinner—made to order. I liked getting to know them. Relationships develop, people keep coming back, and before long, they go from being just a customer to being your friend. (It's actually how I met both my business partner and my wife.) The key is that they start trusting you to serve them whatever you want. When that happens, it really raises your desire to be more creative and make even better food.

It led me to want a whole house for that. To have an entire place where people could come, let their guard down, and let me give them an amazing experience. At Uchi, our primary goal is to accomplish three things:

**1. Satisfy.** People come to Uchi for a certain reason, and we absolutely want to satisfy whatever that expectation might be.

**2. Satiate.** We want to give you something that's the most delicious thing you've ever had. If we just satisfy, that to me is bare minimum. So if you're craving that sushi roll you've had somewhere else, we may have that, but what we give you will be three times better. We want your response to be, "Oh, my God, that's the most incredible thing I've ever put in my mouth!"

**3. Surprise.** There's nothing better than when you're trying new things at a restaurant and pushing your boundaries just a little bit. We want to surprise you with something unexpected, something a little beyond your normal comfort level. By the time you leave, you've had something to remember.

How do we make that happen? We take initiative. All of our staff are trained as if they were individual sushi chefs. We want them asking questions about what a customer likes and what experiences they've had before. Then we want them guiding guests toward something new. You like hamachi sashimi?

Uchi's neta case at the sushi bar is where we store all the items that we put on top of sushi or cut for sashimi. The case is kept at 34° F for absolute freshness. To maintain the best integrity, we never use pre-cut fish. We always keep it in larger pieces, or "saku," until ordered.

You should try the Machi Cure. It's smoked hamachi served with Asian pear, Marcona almonds, crunchy yucca chips, and garlic brittle, and it's amazing. If you typically order spicy tuna roll, you should try the Shag Roll with salmon, sun-dried tomato, and avocado. It's tempura fried and has the same spicy, creamy appeal as the tuna roll.

We also try to bring something from the kitchen that they haven't ordered, more than just an amuse bouche but maybe a special from our menu. That usually takes people a little off guard, but in a good way. People love to feel treated, and receiving a gift from the chef is a great way to make people feel welcome.

A lot of people would say this model is terrible because we give away so much food and therefore money. I don't think that's true. You get customers who can't wait to come back to your restaurant. And they can't wait to bring their friends. It's an investment I'm willing to make. And if you're willing to make an investment in your customers, they're willing to invest in you.

## SETTING THE PACE

Timing is also a key part to our service. There is a rhythm to the way we do things at Uchi. First and foremost, I always want something hitting the table. Part of that is for entertainment value. I don't want people waiting around for the next thing. It's awkward. So when one dish is finished and picked up, BANG—here's the next one. If the server executes it correctly, before you know it, you blink your eyes and you've been sitting there for more than an hour and you've tried 15 different things. It's smooth and seamless, and somehow you don't even know where the time went.

It all stems from my experience on the sushi bar, where I was able to see where my customer was in his meal. When he was finished with one thing, I was ready to give him the next thing. I'm giving him small things, bang, bang, bang, and he's essentially eating out of my hands.

I want every seat at my restaurant to have that sushi bar experience. The only way to do that is to serve smaller portions and deliver things fast. I've trained my staff with those rules and limitations on when they are allowed to "fire" an order. Most sushi restaurants will let the customer order everything all at once.

This is the expo line at the restaurant. We have two expo rails, one for the hot line and one for the sushi line. On most nights these rails are full of tickets before 6:30 p.m.

The problem with that is your sushi line gets one big ticket of sushi to make, which takes a long time and holds up all of the other orders in the restaurant.

Not only are you waiting a long time for food, but the sushi just isn't as good that way. Letting sushi sit on a plate for more than a few minutes degrades the quality of that perfect bite I always talk about. Think about French fries. They are perfect for about seven minutes after they're pulled from the fryer. Wait 30 minutes, and they aren't worth eating. Foods have their window for the perfect bite, and with sushi, it's the second it has been plated. All of the big "sushi boats" you see at other restaurants should be taken out to the ocean and sunk.

We did away with that. Completely. There are no bulk tickets at Uchi. My staff is not allowed to fire more than a couple of orders to the kitchen at once. Even if a table orders 20 items, my wait staff keeps it organized and paced so that it's not even entered for the kitchen until the first few orders have been delivered.

Full disclosure: I'm a total control freak to have it done this way. I realize that. But think about it. When you have a table crowded with a bunch of different plates or, worse, a big humongous sushi boat, you can't focus on what you're eating. You're just cramming things in your mouth. That's not enjoyable. Our way is

more approachable; it's the best way to maintain the integrity of the fish.

**STAFF**

Hospitality is something I want to extend not just to my customers. It also extends to my staff. It's important to establish a culture at a restaurant, not only with your customers but with your staff. If you apply the same sensibilities in hospitality to the people who work for you, they will appreciate that and be happy in their jobs. People who are happy in their jobs will want to come to work and do a good job for you.

In many ways, it's really not about what you create but how you do it. I've figured out a way to run my business from the service to the pacing to the creation of the food, as an extension of my desire to be hospitable. Bottom line: I want everyone to feel like they have been completely taken care of when they visit our restaurant.

UCHI TIPS

**SASHIMI**

When you serve sashimi, the idea is that everything is bite-size, but the size of the slice depends on the amount of fat that the fish has. Lean whitefish such as flounder and striped bass is sliced very thin. But fish from deeper and colder water have more fat and therefore more flavor. So fish such as bluefin tuna and yellowtail should be cut thicker. With sashimi, you always use the best part of the fish to really enhance the flavor of the dish.

FRIDAY, APRIL 9
JI: HORSE MACKEREL
ORO: BLUEFIN BELLY
OQUERONES: SPANISH ANCHOVY
AMA HOTATE: LIVE SCALLOP
ATODAI: JOHN DORY

# MY GREATEST HOPE WITH UCHI IS

TO SHOW MY RESPECT FOR JAPANESE CULTURE THROUGH MY FOOD. I'VE EATEN SUSHI IN JAPAN AND FROM COAST TO COAST IN THE UNITED STATES, AND TO BE HONEST, IT SADDENS ME TO SEE HOW FAR AMERICAN SUSHI FALLS AWAY FROM THE JAPANESE ORIGINAL.

In Japanese, ishi yaki means "cooked on a hot stone." I had ishi yaki for the first time in Tokyo, and I loved how interactive it was. I really wanted this Hot Rock on the Uchi menu. It's one of the most popular dishes for families. Kids love cooking their own food.

I'm the first to admit that America is the land of opportunity. And when it comes to food, this country has made great things out of many different cultural cuisines. But when it comes to sushi, we've butchered it. We've lost the point. When people walk through the doors of my restaurant, my one request is that they put aside what they think they know about sushi and be willing to learn how beautiful and serious this cuisine is.

In Japanese, sushi means "rice with vinegar." It began centuries ago as a way to preserve fish without refrigeration. The main staples of the Japanese diet were rice and fish. Traditionally, the Japanese would cure fish with salt and vinegar to make the fish last longer. Sushi rice is an accent to the fish and is formed in the hand. In fact, that's where the word "nigiri" sushi comes from. It means "by hand." What we know in America as sushi took hundreds of years to evolve. For a long time, sushi rolls in Japan were served at bars and casinos as an easy-to-eat snack, with the seaweed on the outside. To avoid having to use chopsticks or utensils, it was cut into four pieces and eaten with the hands.

If those small tweaks hadn't happened, I don't think the transition to American restaurants would have been as seamless. The cured sushi from centuries ago had such a strong taste that it would never have appealed to the American palate. When Japanese chefs opened sushi bars here in the 1960s, they began paying attention to what Americans liked about it (the delicacy and healthiness) and what they didn't like (the seaweed and raw fish texture). So they began altering things to make them more appetizing. They hid the taste of seaweed by making rolls with rice on the outside. They added sauces like teriyaki and spicy mayonnaise. And they added different textures, like tempura-fried shrimp and vegetables.

Unfortunately, a lot of restaurants are about saving money to make money. That's not always a good thing when it comes to sushi. They'd rather hold on to fish a little longer so they can try to make money on it. Tuna is the biggest casualty of this practice—when you see a spicy tuna roll on special, beware. To charge more for a roll, sushi chefs began making bigger sushi rolls by stuffing more rice and other ingredients inside, as well as by layering ingredients on the outside. Before long, sushi rolls started taking on strange names, like "caterpillar," "dragon," and "rainbow."

But this whole "bigger is better" mentality is ridiculous. You shouldn't be looking for a value menu in which $10 gets you a giant roll that you can't even fit in your mouth. Not only is it disgusting, but you're primarily paying for a lot

of rice and a little bit of fish that may not even be fresh. That's a rip-off. Sushi is a delicacy. It's supposed to be bite-size, and it's supposed to be fresh.

Just as we've done with other cultural foods, we've found a way to Americanize sushi; we've taken it and turned it on its head. In many ways, we've taken the "Japanese" out of it. We put it in grocery stores and order it in restaurants that don't even serve Japanese food. We squirt all sorts of sauces on it and add three times the amount of rice so we can have a more "full" feeling when we're finished. We've "super sized" what is supposed to be a small and delicate food.

To a small extent, I think I'm a part of the evolution of sushi and where it is go-ing. At least, I'm a part of trying to preserve what traditional sushi is about. I'm tak-ing that traditional style and adding to it: something that's a little sexier, something you've probably never tried before. The Japanese have an amazing respect for their food. I hate that we've taken something so simple and pure and messed it up. For that reason, Uchi is about paying respect to the product: using the sharpest knives, keeping things at the right temperature, and giving attention to flavors. Through my restaurants and now this cookbook, I hope to teach people the same reverence that the Japanese have for their cuisine. These people are serious about it. And because of that, I'm serious about it.

My team and I showcased Uchi food at an event dur-ing the early years of the restaurant. Most of these guys are still with me. Masa Saio (third from left) is the head sushi chef at Uchi. Vu Le (far right) is the head sushi chef at our sister restaurant, Uchiko. Paul Qui (second from right) is Uchiko's executive chef and he still collaborates with me on the Uchi menu.

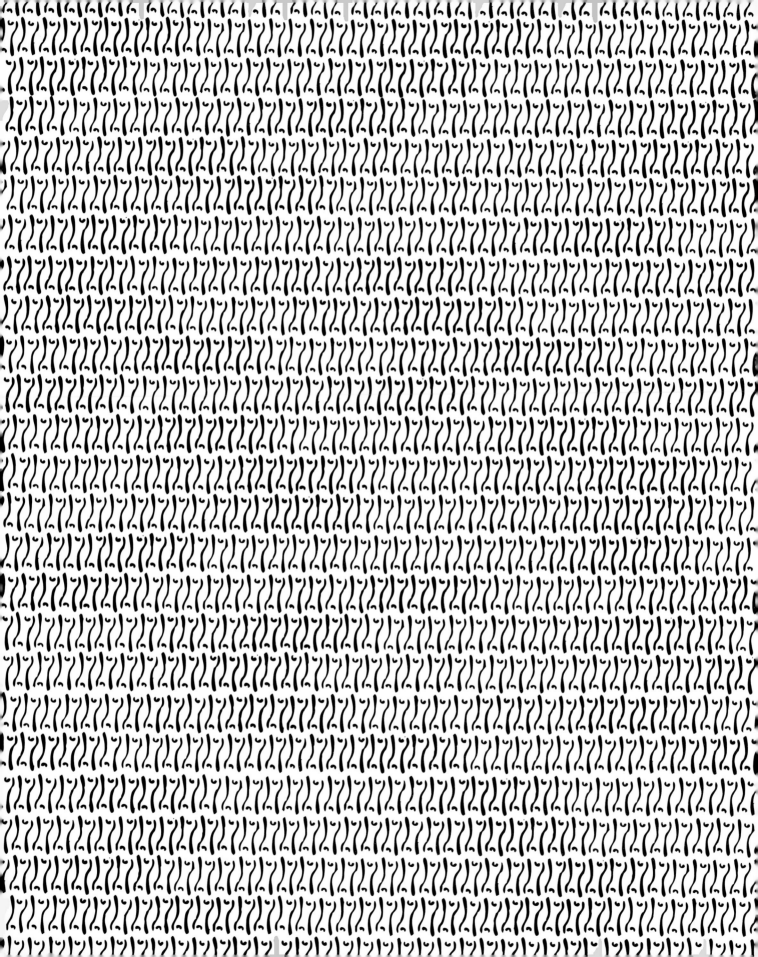

COMPONENTS

# YAKUMI

When I think of our components, I think of the word "yakumi." It means "to stress," "to accentuate something else," "an accessory." In the traditional sushi world, it is something you put on top of the fish as its perfect accent. It could be a sauce or something cut up, like a scallion.

I learned about traditional Japanese yakumi in my training. The Japanese are very strict about specific types of yakumi. Yakumi for tuna is THIS. Yakumi for yellowtail is THIS. There is something specific for every type of fish. In Japan, there's no soy sauce and pickled ginger, so the yakumi for each fish accentuates that particular fish as much as possible.

With Uchi, I wanted to make new yakumi. We considered each cut of fish and asked ourselves what we could do to best complement that fish. For example, garlic candy. To make it, we slice garlic on a mandolin, candy it, and then fry it. Add some dashi, some white soy, and it all comes together to make a delicious new form of yakumi.

In this section, we encourage you to play. Read through the recipes, and you'll see there are things combined in here that we toyed with and perfected, such as corn water and fish caramel. All of these can be used for other dishes as well. And you don't need a lot to make a difference on a dish.

**RECIPE NOTE**

Many of these recipes can be made and reserved for use in other Uchi or Asian-inspired recipes. They are sauces, accents, and various flavor textures that we use for a number of our recipes. Feel free to be creative with these components in your daily cooking. We're always using them to build new recipes at the restaurant.

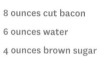

## BACON CANDY

8 ounces cut bacon

6 ounces water

4 ounces brown sugar

Preheat oven to 325° F. It's best to use the thickest cut bacon you can find. If it is possible, use bacon that is not presliced so you can get a nice dice. Cut bacon into ¼-inch dice. In a small sauce pot, bring water and brown sugar to a boil. Let mixture boil for a few minutes to reduce the water content, making it a maple syrup-like consistency. Add diced bacon and cook for about 5 minutes to ensure that the bacon is well coated and the syrup has cooked all the way through the bacon. Strain the bacon out of the sugar-water mixture, place on a silicon mat or a parchment-lined baking tray, and bake for 15 to 20 minutes or until bacon is crispy with a thin, sugary coating.

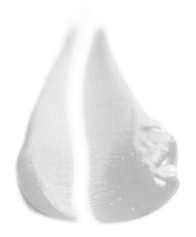

## CANDIED CARROT PURÉE

Peel and wash carrots. Chop carrots in a uniform shape to ensure even cooking. Bring water and brown sugar to a boil. Place chopped carrots into boiling water mixture and cool at a simmer until carrots are fork tender. Remove carrots from liquid and reserve some of the carrot cooking liquid. Place cooked carrots into a blender and begin to pulse, pour about an ounce of cooking liquid into blender, and continue to pulse. Blend until carrots have a uniform puréed consistency. Pour oil into blender and continue to blend to smooth out the purée. Season with salt and pepper, and reserve for use.

24 ounces carrots

16 ounces water

16 ounces brown sugar

2 ounces canola oil

Salt to taste

Fresh ground black pepper

# CANDIED PINE NUT

10 ounces sugar

10 ounces water

16 ounces soybean oil

8 ounces pine nuts

Salt

Bring sugar and water to a boil in a medium saucepan. Meanwhile, heat the soybean oil to 350° F in a separate saucepan. When sugar and water have reached the boiling point, place pine nuts into boiling mixture and cook for 5 minutes at a rolling boil. Remove cooked pine nuts and let them drip off excess water. Transfer pine nuts into heated canola oil and cook until a light golden brown. Remove pine nuts and place in a large stainless bowl. Liberally coat the hot fried pine nuts with salt and spread on a baking sheet to cool. Store candied nuts in an airtight container at room temperature.

# CANDIED TOMATO

Poke small, shallow holes in each stem end of the tomatoes. This will allow the syrup to infuse inside the tomato. Combine water, sugar, and glucose. Heat to a boil and cook until a slight syrupy consistency. Add salt, a pinch of ground black pepper, and vinegar. Mix well and pour hot syrup over tomatoes to begin to cook and candy them. Cover the container with plastic wrap to trap in heat. Let cool to room temperature, and refrigerate to store.

1 pint cherry tomatoes

12 ounces water

8 ounces sugar

3 ounces glucose

Salt to taste

Pinch of black pepper

¼ ounces sherry vinegar

**COMPRESSED COMPONENTS**

Using a vacuum sealer to compress food is a great way to really infuse flavors. For strawberry and watermelon, it almost completely changed the food to something different. Compressing ingredients like this with different flavors not only infuses more depth of flavor but also changes the overall texture.

# COMPRESSED STRAWBERRY

1 pint fresh strawberries

Salt and/or sugar to taste

Thoroughly wash strawberries and remove the tops. Place berries in a large bowl and toss with seasoning. Depending on what the recipe will be used for, berries may be tossed with salt or sugar or both. Also, with this method, you can place a bit of liquid, for example, balsamic vinegar, into the vacuum bag to infuse a flavor. Place seasoned berries into vacuum bag and use vacuum sealer as directed by manufacturer. Compressing the strawberries, with or without seasoning, will intensify the flavor and color of the berry.

# CAULIFLOWER PURÉE

Remove cauliflower pieces from the stalk and chop into uniform 1-inch pieces. Place butter into a cold medium sauté pan and heat up until butter is melted and begins to brown a bit on the sides. Place cauliflower into pan and cook on medium-high heat until tender, about 10 minutes. Once cauliflower is cooked, heat the pan up more on high heat. Deglaze the hot pan with white soy sauce and remove from heat. Place cooked cauliflower into blender and pulse to combine. Once pieces are crumbled, increase blender setting to a medium-high speed and continue to blend until puréed. Incorporate canola oil into the purée, blending for a smooth consistency. Season with salt and pepper to taste.

12 ounces cauliflower

2 ounces butter

1 ounce white soy sauce

2 ounces canola oil

Salt and black pepper
    to taste

# CASHEW BEER BUTTER

If cashews are not purchased preroasted, roast in a 350° F oven until fragrant and dark golden brown. In a blender, combine Dijon, sugar, and salt until well incorporated. Slowly add canola oil to emulsify. While blending, add beer and combine until a smooth purée is achieved. Make sure purée is an even consistency. Reserve at room temperature in an airtight container for later use.

9 ounces roasted cashews

1¼ ounces Dijon mustard

1 ounce sugar

¼ ounce salt

2½ ounces canola oil

12 ounces Asahi dark beer

# COMPRESSED WATERMELON

Depending on what the recipe will be used for, melon may be tossed with salt or sugar or both. Also, with this method, you can place a bit of liquid, such as fish sauce or a pickling liquid, into the vacuum bag to infuse a flavor. Place seasoned watermelon into vacuum bag and use vacuum sealer as directed by manufacturer. Compressing the watermelon, with or without seasoning, will intensify the flavor and color of the melon.

2 pounds watermelon,
    peeled with seeds
    removed

Salt and/or sugar to taste

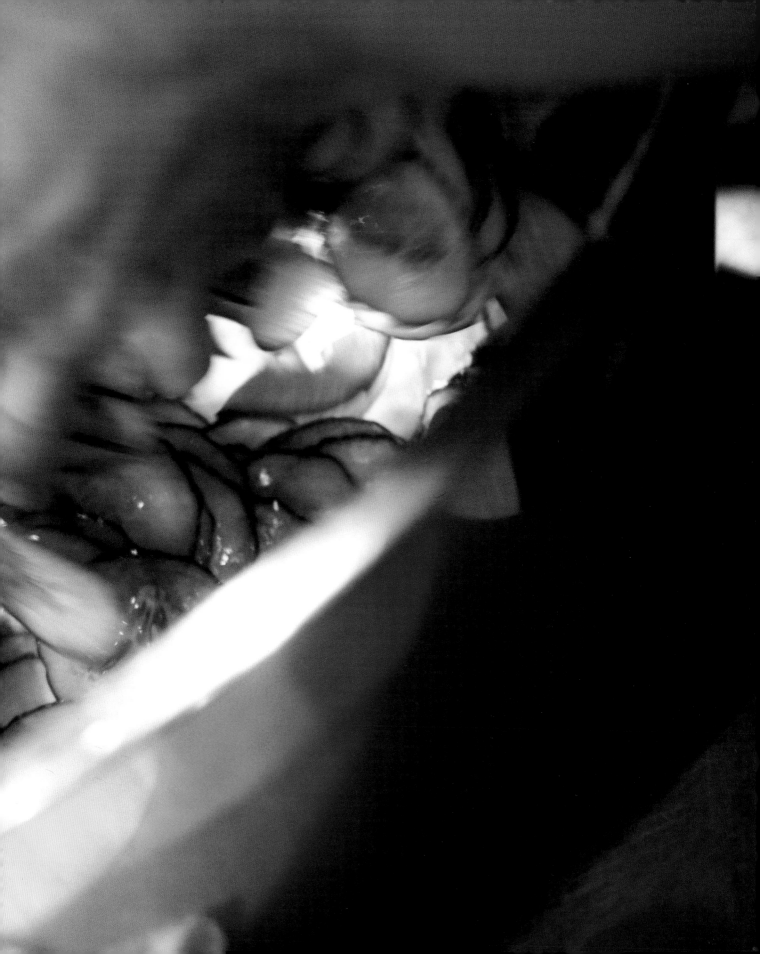

## CUCUMBER GELÉE

Bloom gelatin in ice water for 5 minutes or until soft. Remove gelatin and squeeze out excess water. In a juicer, juice English cucumbers. You should end up with a little more than 12 ounces of cucumber juice. Reserve the juice at room temperature. In a small sauce pot, heat 4 ounces water until just below the boiling point. Remove from heat and add bloomed gelatin. Mix well to combine. Add vinegar and salt to the mixture and stir well to combine. Slowly add the mixture to the cucumber juice while constantly whisking to incorporate. Once well mixed, pour mixture into a small plastic container and refrigerate to set. The gelée will take about 2 hours to set. Cut into desired shapes and reserve in the refrigerator.

4 sheets gelatin

ice water

40 ounces English cucumber

4 ounces water

¼ ounce white vinegar

¼ ounce salt

## ENGLISH PEA PURÉE

Cook peas in salted boiling water until tender and bright green. The peas should not be mushy. Strain them out of the pot and shock in an ice bath. Purée with trimoline inverted sugar and a few ice cubes. Finish purée with olive oil to add smoothness. Season with salt to taste.

1 cup peas

1 cup water

1 teaspoon trimoline
   inverted sugar

1 tablespoon olive oil

Salt to taste

## FISH CARAMEL

Combine first 5 ingredients in a pot and cook to caramelize. Deglaze pan with fish sauce. Add water and sugar and cook until reduced by half, about 30 minutes. Strain, let cool, and reserve for later use.

1 stalk lemongrass,
   rough chopped

1 bulb garlic,
   rough chopped

1 large shallot,
   rough chopped

1 large piece fresh
   ginger, peeled and
   rough chopped

1 Thai chile, rough chopped

1 cup fish sauce

1 cup water

1 cup sugar

## CRISPY QUINOA

Combine water and sugar in a small saucepan over high heat. When mixture comes to a boil, add quinoa and cook until the grain is soft, 12 to 15 minutes. Drain quinoa. Heat up oil in frying pan. Add quinoa and fry until dark golden brown. Strain from oil and season with salt.

1 cup water

¼ cup sugar

¼ cup quinoa

1 cup soybean oil

2 teaspoons salt

# FISH SAUCE GELÉE

Bloom gelatin sheets in ice water for about 5 minutes or until soft. Remove gelatin and squeeze off excess water. Reserve for later use. Strain fish sauce and gently heat 2 cups over medium-high heat until just before the boiling point. Remove from heat and place bloomed gelatin into sauce. Mix well to fully incorporate the gelatin. Pour through a fine mesh sieve. Pour mixture onto a flat baking tray and refrigerate to set, about 4 hours. Cut into desired pieces.

4 sheets gelatin

Ice water

2 cups strained Uchi fish
    sauce (See page 80
    for recipe.)

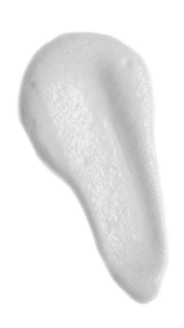

# FRIED APPLE PURÉE

Peel and cut apples into large uniform chunks. Heat oil over medium heat and add chopped apples. Add the sugar and coat the apples. Let cook until apples are soft, 5 to 7 minutes. Remove apples from oil and place into a blender. Reserve the oil. Add water to the apples and blend to a uniform consistency. Slowly add reserved oil to emulsify and blend until smooth. Reserve at room temperature for later use.

2 large Granny Smith
    apples

4 ounces vegetable oil

2 ounces sugar

4 ounces water

# FRIED EGG PURÉE

¼ ounce butter

2 eggs

2 ounces water

Salt and ground black
    pepper to taste

2 ounces canola oil

Heat butter over medium heat in a small sauté pan. Once the butter has been melted through and the pan is well heated, crack eggs into pan and fry them over easy, just enough to cook the whites through. Remove eggs from pan and place into blender. Blend on low speed until puréed into a uniform consistency. Add water to break up eggs and continue to blend to form a smooth purée with a thin consistency. Add salt and ground black pepper to taste, and finish purée by slowly adding the canola oil while blending. Once well mixed, the purée should have a consistency similar to that of mayonnaise. Remove from blender and store in refrigerater for later use.

# GARLIC CANDY

Peel whole cloves of garlic. Slice garlic paper thin on a mandolin or with a very sharp knife. Quickly blanch sliced garlic in a pot of boiling water for no more than 30 seconds. Remove garlic from boiling water and repeat step in the second pot of boiling water. Bring sugar and water to a boil in separate medium saucepan. Remove garlic from blanching water and place into boiling sugar and water mixture. Reduce heat and let garlic chips cook at a simmer for about 10 minutes or until translucent in color. In a high-sided sauté pan, heat canola oil to 325° F and reserve at that temperature for frying. Remove garlic from syrup and rinse in a strainer to remove excess syrup. Shake off excess water and place in heated oil. Fry until light golden brown. Reserve in an airtight container for later use as a garnish.

2 heads garlic

2 pots of boiling water

24 ounces sugar

8 ounces water

24 ounces canola oil

## GRILLED GARLIC PURÉE

Toss peeled garlic cloves with 1 ounce oil and liberally season with salt. Grill seasoned garlic on the hot part of the grill. (Char the outside for the best effect.) Flip the garlic and continue to grill on a cooler part of the grill. Continue to cook until garlic becomes slightly tender to the touch, about 5 minutes. Let garlic cool to room temperature and place in a blender. Add water and begin to purée. Add the vinegar, salt, and pepper. Once the purée has reached a smooth uniform consistency, gently stream in the remaining oil to finish the purée. The oil will thicken up the purée and give it a nice sheen. Taste again and reseason to taste. Store in an airtight container in the refrigerator.

3 ounces garlic cloves, peeled (about 4 heads garlic)

6 ounces vegetable oil

Kosher salt to taste

4 ounces water

½ ounce sherry vinegar

Ground black pepper to taste

## GOMA SHIO

Preheat oven to 325° F. Toast sesame seeds in oven until fragrant and a light golden brown. Let seeds cool. Mix seeds with kosher salt and grind coarsely in a food processor until well combined. Reserve at room temperature for later use.

2 ounces white sesame seeds

1 ounce kosher salt

## HEIRLOOM TOMATO WATER

28 ounces ripe heirloom tomatoes

½ ounce kosher salt

½ ounce sugar

2 ounces water

In a food processor, pulse tomatoes until they are roughly chopped, 5 to 6 pulses. (You do not want to purée the tomatoes as it will cause the water to color.) Toss the processed tomatoes with salt and sugar, and place into a fine mesh sieve that has been lined with 2 or 3 layers of cheesecloth. Place the sieve in a large bowl and pour the water over the tomatoes. The salt and sugar will help to pull juices from the tomatoes. Let the tomatoes sit overnight in the refrigerator to extract all the juices. The tomato water will drain, and the result should be clear, similar to water, with a yellowish tint. This recipe yields about 12 ounces of tomato water.

## HAZELNUT BUTTER

Preheat oven to 350° F. In a small saucepan, combine sugar and water and cook over medium heat. Cook until the caramelized stage, just as the edges are beginning to turn a golden brown. Remove from heat and let sit for about a minute to let the sugar continue to cook. Pour sugar onto a silicon mat or a parchment-lined baking tray, and spread as thinly as possible. Toast hazelnuts in the oven until golden brown, about 12 minutes. While hazelnuts are still hot, grind in food processor until they reach a pasty consistency. Add salt and continue to blend until the mixture resembles peanut butter. Add the caramelized sugar and continue to blend until well incorporated. Remove from food processor and store in an airtight container at room temperature.

4 ounces sugar

2 ounces water

8 ounces hazelnuts, peeled and blanched

¼ ounce kosher salt

# JASMINE WATER SORBET

In a large sauce pot, combine first 4 ingredients. Heat mixture over medium heat until it reaches the boiling point. Remove mixture from heat and add jasmine water extract. Cool sorbet mixture over an ice bath. Freeze in an ice cream machine according to manufacturer's instructions.

32 ounces water

8 ounces sugar

4 ounces glucose syrup

2 ounces sorbet stabilizer

6 ounces jasmine
   water extract*

*Jasmine water extract can be found in specialty food stores and Asian markets.*

## KUMQUAT CONFIT

Slice kumquats thinly on the cross section and reserve. Combine the water, sugar, glucose, and vinegar in a small saucepan and bring to the boiling point. Add the citric acid and salt, and stir. Add the kumquats. As the seeds float to the top, remove them. Reduce heat to medium-low and continue to cook until the skins become translucent and the liquid is of a thick syrup-like consistency. Remove from heat and reserve at room temperature.

2 ounces kumquats

4 ounces water

2 ounces sugar

1 ounce glucose syrup

¼ ounce white vinegar

1 pinch citric acid

Kosher salt to taste

## KATSUOBUSHI SORBET

In a large sauce pot, combine water, sugar, and glucose syrup. Heat mixture over medium heat until it reaches the boiling point. Remove mixture from heat and add Katsuobushi. Make sure all the flakes are submerged in the mixture. Let flakes steep for about 10 minutes. Strain entire mixture through a fine mesh sieve and cool over an ice bath. Freeze in an ice cream machine according to manufacturer's instructions.

32 ounces water

8 ounces sugar

4 ounces glucose syrup

1 ounce katsuobushi

   (bonito flakes)

# LEMON PURÉE

Peel the lemons. Reserve the center meat for juicing, and use the peels to simmer in water with sugar. When the peels are tender to the touch, almost falling apart, remove and place in blender to purée. Combine lemon juice and simple syrup. Use that mixture to loosen the purée while it's blending. You want to use just enough to get the lemon rinds mixing. Emulsify with canola oil to custard-like consistency, and salt to taste. Refrigerate for later use.

*For simple syrup, combine equal parts water and sugar in a small sauce pot. Heat until sugar dissolves completely. Let cool, and reserve for use.*

6 lemons

2 quarts water

16 ounces sugar

4 ounces lemon juice

4 ounces simple syrup*

2 ounces canola oil

Salt to taste

# KIMCHEE BASE

Peel and grate ginger, and reserve in a small bowl. With a sharp knife, slice garlic into paper thin rounds, place into separate container, and reserve. With a sharp knife, slice shallot into thin rounds, ⅛ inch. Slice negi whites and greens into 1-inch pieces. Heat a saucepan on high heat, add canola oil, and let heat until near smoking point. Add ingredients, one at a time in this order: shallot, garlic, ginger, negi whites, and negi greens. Cook each ingredient, one at a time, for about a minute each. Keep pan hot and keep the ingredients moving around, similar to a stir fry. Add sesame oil and sugar, and continue to cook until sugar dissolves. Remove from heat and let cool to room temperature. Add fish sauce and salt, and mix well.

1 ounce ginger

1 ounce garlic

1 ounce shallot

4 ounces negi whites
(green onion)

2 ounces negi greens

1 ounce canola oil

1½ ounces sesame oil

1 ounce sugar

¼ ounce Korean red
pepper flake

3 ounces fish sauce

Salt to taste

# NORI PURÉE

Soak nori sheets in water to rehydrate them; they will become loose and pliable. Purée the nori with the soaking liquid and white soy sauce. Mix until well combined with a consistent texture. The nori will look a bit pasty. Finish the purée by drizzling canola oil into the mixture until a nice, smooth purée forms. Reserve in an airtight container for later use.

10 sheets nori

8 ounces water

1 ounces white soy

3 ounces canola oil,

approximately

# NECTARINE BUTTER

Remove nectarines from pit and slice into 1-inch slices. Coat with olive oil and lightly season with salt. Place seasoned nectarines onto hot part of grill and let char on one side. Flip nectarines, move them to a cooler part of the grill, and let cook through until tender. Remove from grill and let cool to room temperature. In a food processor, place nectarines, butter, and salt together. Purée to a smooth consistency. Reserve at room temperature for later use.

5 ounces nectarines

(about 2 nectarines)

Drizzle of olive oil

Salt to taste

5 ounces butter

¼ ounces salt

# MEYER LEMON THYME VINAIGRETTE

Mix together lemon juice, sugar, thyme, salt, and pepper in a medium bowl. In a separate bowl, mix together both oils and slowly whisk into lemon juice mixture. Refrigerate in airtight container to store.

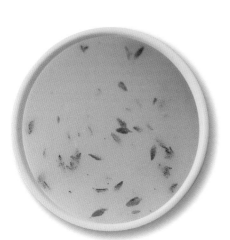

8 ounces lemon juice

6 ounces sugar

½ ounce picked thyme

leaves

¼ ounce salt

½ teaspoon fresh ground

black pepper

10 ounces vegetable oil

2 ounces olive oil

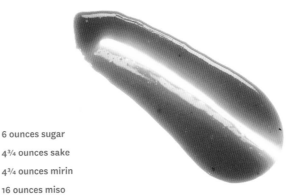

6 ounces sugar

4¾ ounces sake

4¾ ounces mirin

16 ounces miso

# MISO BASE

Combine sugar, sake, and mirin, bring to a boil, and reduce by ¼ over medium heat. Add miso and mix well. Continue to cook over medium heat until dark in color. Stir often so that bottom does not burn. Chill over ice bath and refrigerate for later use.

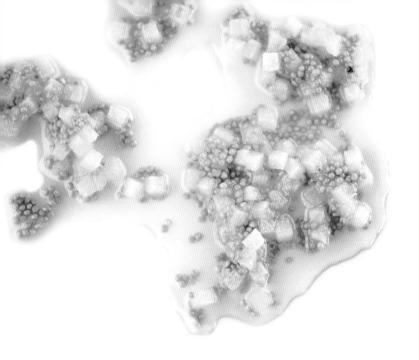

## PEAR MOSTARDA

In a medium saucepan, simmer the pear in white wine and sugar. In a small pot, bring salted water to a boil and blanch the mustard seeds twice to decrease intensity of flavor, about 5 minutes each time. Add blanched mustard seeds to the pear mixture. Add the rapid-set pectin and cook on medium-low heat, stirring until the mostarda thickens. Reserve in refrigerator for later use.

1 Asian pear, peeled and
   small diced

1 cup white wine

½ cup sugar

4 ounces mustard seeds

1 teaspoon rapid-set pectin

## PICKLED QUAIL EGGS

Bring a pot of salted water to a boil. Gently place quail eggs into boiling water and let cook for 2 minutes. Immediately place cooked eggs into an ice bath. Once cooled, peel eggs. In a medium bowl, marinate peeled eggs in sushi zu mixture for 3 minutes. Remove from sushi zu and reserve in refrigerator for later use.

1 dozen quail eggs

1 cup sushi zu

   (See page 79 for recipe.)

# OLIVE CANDY

Remove olives from brine and use a kitchen towel to wring out excess moisture. In a dehydrator dry olives until they are brittle, or place olives overnight in a gas oven with the pilot light on or in an electric oven set to 100° F. Once olives are fully dehydrated and brittle, reserve for later use in the recipe. Place sugar into a small, heavy-bottomed saucepan and evenly moisten the sugar with the water. Cook sugar to the point of caramelizing. The edges of the sugar should start turning a golden color. Remove from heat and let the residual heat continue to cook the sugar, about 1 minute. Place olives on a silicon mat or a piece of parchment paper. Pour cooked sugar over them and let the sugar harden as it cools, at room temperature. In a food processor, coarsely grind olives and caramelized sugar. Reserve in an airtight container and leave at room temperature.

*Never refrigerate caramelized sugar. It will begin to sweat, which will make your caramel chewy and not crispy.*

8 ounces kalamata olives

16 ounces sugar

4 ounces water

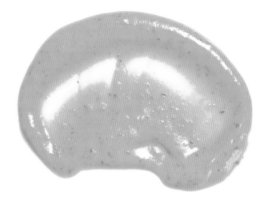

# PEACH KIMCHEE EMULSION

Place the kimchee base and chopped peaches into a blender, and purée to combine until smooth. Slowly pour in olive oil to emulsify and season with kosher salt to taste. Remove from blender and reserve for use.

2 ounces kimchee base
   (See page 67 for recipe.)

4 ounces fresh peaches,*
   chopped

2 ounces high-quality extra
   virgin olive oil

Kosher salt to taste

*You may substitute
canned peaches if fresh
peaches are not available.*

# SUGAR CURE

Place salt and sugar in large mixing bowl.
Combine cinnamon sticks, cloves, and juniper
berries in a kitchen towel and crush with the
back of a knife. Grind in a spices grinder until coarsely ground. Combine spices with sugar
and salt mixture. Reserve at room temperature
in an airtight container.

4 ounces kosher salt

12 ounces sugar

2 cinnamon sticks

2 teaspoons cloves

2 teaspoons juniper berries

COMPONENTS

**MISE EN PLACE**

The most important thing in a restaurant kitchen is the mise en place. It's all of those ingredients that accentuate the dishes you're making. There is a lot of prep work involved for this, but you must have every ingredient in order before you can really begin any type of cooking. At Uchi, we always have someone dedicated specifically to the mise en place, from the timing or preparation and the required temperatures for everything to making sure ingredients are replenished as needed.

# SHIITAKE BACON

Slice shiitake mushroom caps ⅛ inch in width. Slowly heat canola oil to about 275° F, place sliced shiitake mushroom caps into heated oil, and let slowly fry until a dark golden color. Pieces should be crispy and somewhat translucent. Season with salt and togarashi spice while warm.

2 ounces shiitake mushrooms
   (weight with stems
   removed)
16 ounces canola oil
Kosher salt and togarashi*
   spice to taste

*Togarashi spice is
available at most Asian
markets.*

# PRESERVED LEMON

Slice lemons crosswise to ⅛ inch in thickness, to resemble wheels. Mix salt and sugar together and toss lemon slices in mixture. Place sliced lemons into a vacuum seal bag and pour remaining salt/sugar mixture into the bag. Vacuum and seal according to manufacturer's instructions, and let preserve for at least 1 hour. Remove from bag and reserve for later use.

2 lemons

4 ounces kosher salt

4 ounces sugar

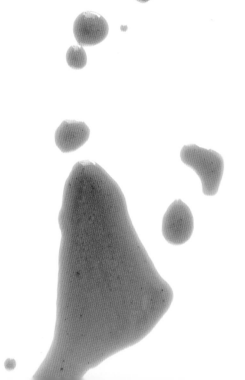

# PITCHFORK SAUCE

1 Thai chile

2 cloves garlic

5 ounces prepared miso base
   (See page 69 for recipe.)

¾ ounce tamari

½ teaspoon egg yolk

Mince Thai chile. (You may remove seeds to make less spicy.) Peel garlic cloves and mince. Add garlic and chile to the miso base and combine well. Add tamari and continue to mix well. Let mixture sit overnight to infuse flavors of the garlic and Thai chile. After the sauce has infused, strain it through a fine mesh sieve to remove pieces. With a handheld blender, finish the sauce by adding egg yolk and mixing well to smooth out purée.

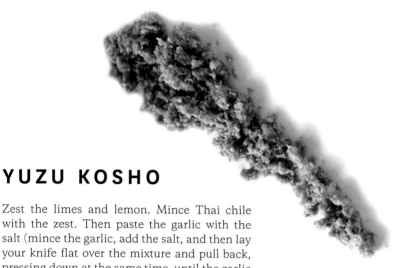

## YUZU KOSHO

Zest the limes and lemon. Mince Thai chile with the zest. Then paste the garlic with the salt (mince the garlic, add the salt, and then lay your knife flat over the mixture and pull back, pressing down at the same time, until the garlic forms a paste). Now fold together the zest and chile mixture with the garlic paste, and mince until well combined.

10 limes

1 lemon

¼ ounce Thai chiles

4 cloves garlic

2 teaspoons kosher salt

## SUNCHOKE CHIPS

Peel sunchokes with a mandolin or very sharp knife. Slice sunchokes paper thin, and place into a high-sided container. In a small pot, bring about a pint of water to a rolling boil. Pour the boiling water over the sliced sunchokes. Let the sunchokes cook in hot water for about 10 minutes or until tender. Strain out the water. In a small saucepan heat canola oil to 300° F. Fry sunchoke slices, a few at a time, until they reach a golden brown color. Remove chips from fryer and lightly season with kosher salt. Reserve in an airtight container for later use.

12 ounces sunchoke

   (Jerusalem artichoke)

6 ounces canola oil

Kosher salt to taste

## UNI BUTTER

Rinse fresh uni in cold water to remove any sand or grit. In a blender, purée uni and yuzu juice until well combined. Add salt and water, and continue to blend until smooth consistency. Gently stream in the canola oil and mix until a uniform texture. Remove from blender and refrigerate for later use.

5 ounces fresh, live uni

1½ ounces fresh yuzu juice

¼ ounce salt

1¾ ounces water

5 ounces canola oil

## SATSUMAIMO BUTTER

Preheat oven to 375° F. Lightly salt satsumaimo and wrap in aluminum foil with 3 ounces butter, and roast for about an hour or until fork tender. Remove from oven and reserve in foil to cool down. Cut remaining butter into cubes. In a small sauce pot, heat water until just before boiling point, remove from heat, and briskly whisk in butter until well combined. When potato is cooled enough to handle, but still warm, pass through a potato ricer or a tammi. (Try to use as little force and motion as possible. If you use too much, it will overwork the potato, which will leave your result gummy.) Return sauce pot to heat. Use a wooden spoon to mount the passed potato into the warm butter and water mixture. Stir over low heat until well combined. Remove from heat and reserve at room temperature for later use.

10 ounces roasted satsumaimo

   (Japanese sweet potato)

½ ounce salt

3 ounces plus 10 ounces

   unsalted butter

2 ounces water

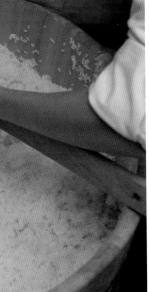

# SUSHI RICE

Wash rice until the water runs clear, about 5 times rinsing and draining. The first wash should use the most vigorous agitation. Allow water to drain for a few minutes after the fifth wash. Place washed rice into rice cooker. Allow to soak for 20 minutes or until all the grains have turned white. Place cap on rice cooker and start cooking according to manufacture's directions. Prepare sushi zu, wet linen, spatula, and large stainless steel bowl. When rice has been cooked, transfer into large stainless bowl. Pour sushi zu onto wooden rice paddle or plastic spatula. "Cut" rice with spatula, distributing rice while incorporating sushi zu evenly throughout. Move rice onto side of bowl and repeat cutting. Move all the rice onto side using damp linen drizzled with rice wine vinegar. Again, cut rice until rice has cooled.

4 cups koshi hikari
   (sushi rice)
4 cups water
2 ounces sushi zu

**SUSHI RICE**

When I first learned to make sushi rice, I was using a wooden paddle and a fan to infuse the vinegar into the hot rice quickly. The key to perfect sushi rice is that the temperature must be consistent. But when the fan is blowing the top of the rice, the rice underneath is still very hot. So you're constantly folding it to bring the hot rice to the top, but you can get only so much consistency with the wooden paddle. So I started wrapping towels with a little vinegar on them around my hands and folding the rice with my hands. That way, I could actually feel when the temperature was consistent.

# SUSHI ZU

2 ounces kombu seaweed*
8 ounces rice wine vinegar
8 ounces sugar

*Kombu seaweed may be
found at Asian markets.*

Wipe kombu with wet paper towel until all salt sediment has been removed. Whisk remaining ingredients together in a small sauce pot over medium-low heat until sugar has dissolved. Let the kombu steep for 10 minutes before removing. Refrigerate sushi zu for later use.

COMPONENTS

## SAN BAI ZU

Heat water and sugar to just below boiling point and then remove from heat. Add hon dashi and mix well to dissolve. Next, add soy and rice wine vinegar. Mix well and refrigerate for later use.

2 ounces water

¼ ounce sugar

1 pinch hon dashi*

¼ ounce soy sauce

2¼ ounces rice wine vinegar

*Hon dashi is a type of Japanese fish soup stock that can be found at most Asian food markets.*

8 ounces soy sauce

12 ounces water

½ teaspoon yuzu kosho
    (See page 76 for recipe.)

2 ounces rice wine vinegar

¼ ounce macadamia oil

¼ ounce sesame oil

2 ounces yuzu juice

1 ounce negi (green onion)
    stalks (whites),
    sliced thinly

## SABAZU

Combine all ingredients in medium bowl. Refrigerate for later use.

## YUZU PON

Combine all ingredients. Mix well and refrigerate for later use.

4 ounces soy sauce

4 ounces white distilled
    vinegar

4 ounces water

¼ ounce fresh yuzu juice

## UCHI FISH SAUCE

Combine garlic, shallots, ginger, chile, and cilantro. In a large metal mixing bowl, combine the garlic mixture with water, lime juice, sugar, and fish sauce. Mix well. Reserve without straining to let flavors infuse. Refrigerate for later use.

1 ounce garlic, peeled and
    rough chopped

1 ounce shallot, peeled and
    rough chopped

½ ounce fresh ginger, peeled
    and grated

¼ ounce Thai chile, chopped

1 ounce cilantro, chopped

18 ounces water

9½ ounces fresh squeezed
    lime juice

9 ounces sugar

5¼ ounces fish sauce
    (recommend Squid brand
    fish sauce)

UCHI TIPS

FISH SAUCE

There are two main kinds of fish sauce, Thai and Vietnamese, and they're really different. Thai style is a little bit stronger and darker. Vietnamese is a little lighter. They're both made from fermented fish. I prefer the Vietnamese style, where they mix it and add chiles, garlic, spice, and citrus to the actual sauce when they're preparing food. The Uchi fish sauce is similar to that. It's great on a lot of things including fish, but it's also fantastic with meat and chicken.

UCHI, THE COOKBOOK

80

SUSHI ZU

SAN BAI ZU

YUZU PON

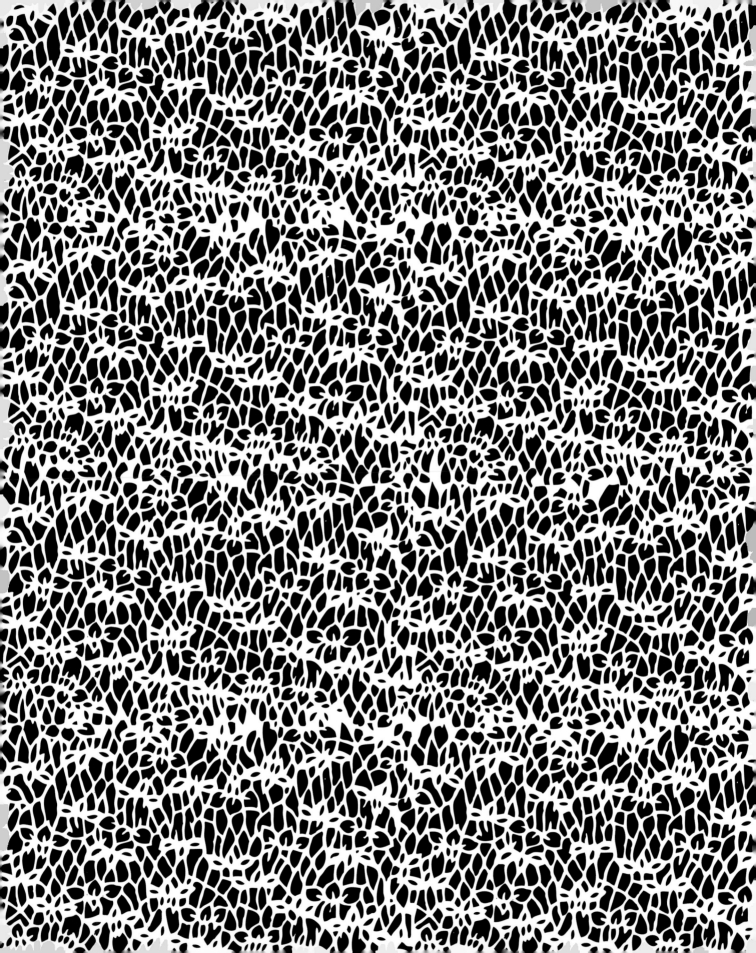

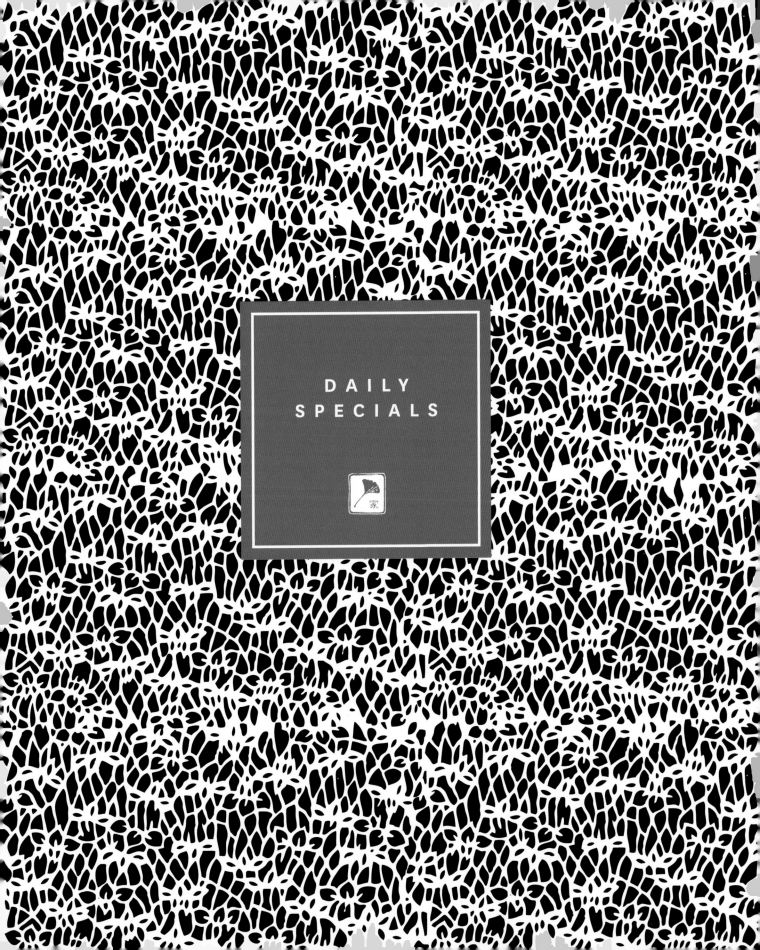

DAILY
SPECIALS

# CHASING THE NEW

The point of Daily Specials is to have a rotating menu. A lot of restaurants have one menu that changes every day, which works well for some places. To me, the problem with that concept is that it's hard to be consistent. You're always making something new. And although new is intriguing, a lot of people who go to a restaurant and have something great want to go back and have it again. If you look at the other side of the coin, chain concepts that are standardized have one menu that's there forever and doesn't change. So if you have something that you really like, it's always going to be there. That presents a lot of value.

With Uchi, I wanted to do both. I wanted to do seasonal things with new, incredible products to play with, but I also wanted some of our offerings to be permanent. So we split the menu in two. Half of the menu is a list of hot and cold tastings and a lineup of sushi and rolls that remain semipermanent, and the other half of the menu is the Daily Specials, which change, well, daily.

The Daily Specials are really a creative canvas for my team, Paul Qui, Philip Speer, and me. It's our way of taking what's best about Japanese food and tweaking it just a little bit to make it even better. We always want to push the boundaries a little bit and stay current with our food.

To do that well, you have to have an arsenal of ingredients. When Uchi first opened, I struggled to get purveyors to give me what I wanted at a decent quantity and price. But once business picked up, they started to believe in what we were doing, and now vendors from everywhere are calling us with their fresh catch of the day, asking if we want it.

I love it. It gives me the ability to be creative but also to teach and mentor my staff throughout the process. I love to come up with ideas with them and then challenge them to develop something based on certain parameters. They always come back with something amazing, and then we edit things down, asking questions like, "Does it have the right texture?" "Does it have enough acid?" "Does it have the right amount of spice?"

All of that can take a day or two before we're ready to introduce it to the Daily Specials menu, but it's worth it to take the time and get it right.

**PAUL QUI**

I owe much of the creativity of our Daily Specials to Paul Qui, my longtime chef de cuisine, who is now running our sister restaurant, Uchiko, as executive chef. He started at the Texas Culinary Academy. We had him stage at Uchi for a few months before I realized how talented he really was. He has a passion that you just can't teach. He quickly worked through all of our stations, from prep and pantry to desserts and grill.

Working side by side with Paul, I realized he was "the guy." I had worked with a number of chefs over the years, but he was the one person who could take something I had shown him or an idea that I was playing with and bring it to fruition. He'd get really excited about it, and a day or two later he would come back to me with that same idea, only three times better.

At first I felt really threatened. I thought, "Man, this guy's really good." And then I realized what a great compliment that is. What's the problem with that? It's great! When you can teach someone something and they can make it better, then you're able to learn from them too. I knew I needed to give him everything he needed to continue to be great.

Over the course of three years, he worked his way up through the stages of our sushi bar. He kept graduating levels, and I kept wanting to promote him. He became my sous chef and then my chef de cuisine. And through all of that time, I have to say, Paul remains one of the most humble people I've ever met. He really wants to do the best he can. He's all about the food, and he has the perfect combination of right- and left-brain qualities that make a really great chef.

The funny thing is, he's so passionate and so serious about the food that he's gotten into a rhythm of wanting things done a certain way. He's very particular. I think I may have created a monster through Paul, but I wouldn't have it any other way.

**RECIPE NOTE**

These recipes are designed for a single plating with multiple bites rather than designated to serve a certain quantity of people (i.e. Serves 6). At Uchi, our dishes are plated and served with the intention that they are shared at a table. Recipes can be adjusted if you are serving a large number of people.

# AKAMI TE *TUNA MERON*

THIS IS ACTUALLY SOMETHING I CAME UP WITH AT THE VERY BEGIN-NING. UCHI HAD BARELY OPENED, AND I WAS STILL ON THE SUSHI LINE. I WAS TOYING AROUND WITH TUNA AND WATERMELON. THE TWO COL-ORS ARE ALMOST IDENTICAL AND, AMAZINGLY, THEIR FLAVORS JUST BURST WHEN YOU PUT THEM TOGETHER—ESPECIALLY WITH THE FISH SAUCE AND A LITTLE SALT. IT'S ONE OF THE TOP BEST BITES YOU CAN MAKE. A REALLY COLD MELON. SOME REALLY GREAT TUNA. THEY'RE JUST MEANT TO BE TOGETHER.

2 ounces fresh tuna loin

*FISH SAUCE FLUID GEL*

⅛ ounce agar agar

4 ounces water

8 ounces prepared
    fish sauce

Salt to taste

*HERB PURÉE*

3 garlic cloves

1 whole shallot

6 ounces vegetable oil

kosher salt

½ ounce cilantro leaves

½ ounce mint leaves

½ ounce basil leaves

*COMPRESSED
WATERMELON*

(See page 55 for recipe.)

*GARNISH*

Kosher salt

Olive oil

Mint leaves

Cilantro leaves

Basil leaves

Fresh cracked black pepper

**FOR THE FISH SAUCE FLUID GEL:** In a medium-size sauce pot, sprinkle the agar agar on top of the water and let it sit for 5 minutes to bloom. Place the agar and water mixture over medium-high heat. Cook the mixture until it comes to a boil, while constantly stirring. Once the mixture has reached a boil, continue to cook while vigorously mixing for 1 additional minute. Remove from heat and whisk in the prepared fish sauce. Salt to taste. Pour into a plastic container and refrigerate to set for about 1 hour. Once the mixture has set, place into a blender and blend on high until the gel is a fluid consistency. Remove from blender and refrigerate until ready for use.

**FOR THE HERB PURÉE:** Peel and rough chop garlic and shallots to a uniform size. In a small sauté pan gently sweat garlic and shallots in about 1 ounce of vegetable oil over low heat. Add a pinch of kosher salt to help bring the flavors from the garlic and shallot. While garlic is heating, bring a small sauce pot of salted water to a boil. Prepare an ice bath for shocking the herbs after they are blanched. Quickly blanch cilantro leaves in boiling water for about 30 seconds, and then immediately shock the cilantro in the prepared ice bath. Repeat this method with the mint and basil leaves. Remove from ice bath and place on paper towels to soak up excess water. Place sweated shallot and garlic, with cooking oil, into a stainless bowl and place on ice bath to cool down. In a blender, purée remaining oil and prepared ingredients. Try to keep oil as cool as possible while blending. This will keep it from turning color. Once all ingredients are consistently puréed, remove from blender and cool down again on ice bath. Reserve herb purée at room temperature for later use.

**ASSEMBLY:** Slice the tuna against the grain into 6 thin slices using a very sharp knife. (Reserve the tuna in a stainless bowl with plastic wrap placed over it in the refrigerator to keep it as cold as possible.) In a small chilled stainless steel bowl, toss the tuna and the compressed watermelon with a generous pinch of kosher salt and about a ¼ ounce of high-quality fruity olive oil. Place the tuna, end over end, across a shallow rimmed round chilled plate. Place cubes of the compressed watermelon around the portioned tuna. With a spoon, streak the plate with the herb purée and place small pools of the purée around the tuna and watermelon. Place about 6 small pools of the fish sauce fluid gel in between the watermelon and purée. Finish the plate with herb leaves—fresh mint, cilantro, and basil—and sprinkle a small amount of fresh-cracked black pepper on top of the fish and melon. Serve immediately.

# AO SABA

## *SABA, JUNIPER, ONION, HUCKLEBERRY BOSHI*

MACKEREL IS SOMETHING I FELL IN LOVE WITH WHEN I LEARNED HOW TO EAT SUSHI. IT'S PROBABLY THE FIFTH OR SIXTH PHASE OF SUSHI WHEN LEARNING TO APPRECIATE THIS CUISINE. ONCE YOU'RE TO THE SASHIMI STAGE, YOU'RE ON TO THE "TRYING OTHER FISH" STAGE. MACKEREL IS USUALLY FISHY AND SOMETIMES FATTY. IT'S DEFINITELY AN ACQUIRED TASTE. THE SAUCE HAS FRESH HUCKLEBERRIES THAT ARE MACERATED AFTER THEY'VE BEEN CURED WITH SALT. IT WAS ENTIRELY PAUL QUI'S IDEA TO CREATE THIS BOSHI, AND IT IS AMAZING WITH THIS FISH. THE IDEA WAS TO REALLY PUSH THE FLAVOR HERE AND CREATE THE CONCEPT OF UMAMI. IT MAKES SOMETHING THAT WOULDN'T BE AS ACCESSIBLE BEFORE MUCH MORE APPROACHABLE.

### PICKLED BLUE FOOT MUSHROOMS
6 ounces white vinegar
6 ounces sugar
12 ounces water
4 ounces blue foot mushrooms

### HUCKLEBERRY GASTRIQUE
4½ ounces water
½ ounce yukari
3½ ounces sugar
4 ounces huckleberry
Kosher salt

### SABA SHIME
4 ounces saba fillet
4 ounces salt
2½ ounces dried kombu
8 ounces rice wine vinegar

### TOASTED JUNIPER
2 ounces dried juniper berries

### GARNISH
Borage blossoms

**FOR THE BLUE FOOT MUSHROOMS:** Combine first 3 ingredients into a medium sauce pot and bring to a boil to dissolve sugar. Place quartered or halved mushrooms in hot liquid. Remove from heat and allow to cool. Reserve for grilling. Before serving, sear the mushrooms on the hot part of a grill to lightly char.

**FOR THE HUCKLEBERRY GASTRIQUE:** Combine water, yukari, and sugar in a small sauce pot. Mix well and bring to a boil. Simmer until the liquid coats the back of a spoon. Remove from heat, add the huckleberries, and mix well. Adjust the taste with kosher salt if necessary. Let cool to room temperature and reserve until use.

**FOR THE SABA SHIME:** Place the cleaned saba fillet, flesh side down, in salt. The salt should cover the whole flesh side of fish. Let the fillet cure for 30 minutes. Remove from the salt and carefully rinse off the salt with cold water. You must be gentle as saba flesh is very fragile. Wipe off white sediment from kombu with a damp cloth. Place the whole fillet in a container and cover with rice wine vinegar and dried kombu. Soak in mixture for 1 hour. Remove fish and place onto clean, lint-free kitchen towel. With skin side up, gently peel off outer skin, starting at the belly side of the fish. Score the skin side in a small crisscross pattern and reserve fish in the refrigerator until use.

**FOR THE TOASTED JUNIPER:** Preheat oven to 325° F. Place the berries on a quarter sheet tray and toast in the oven for 10 to 15 minutes. Crush with the back of a knife to get a rough crumb. Reserve in an airtight container for use.

**ASSEMBLY:** On a small rectangular plate, run a line of huckleberry gastrique down the center, with two pools at either end. One should be larger than the other. Place the grilled pickled mushrooms off-center near the larger pool of sauce. Place seared fish on top of mushrooms. Garnish with borage blossoms and two piles of toasted juniper berries.

# BACON SEN
## *ROASTED PORK BELLY, FRIED APPLE PURÉE*

THIS IS ONE OF MANY ITERATIONS WE HAD FOR PORK BELLY AT UCHI. AT THE VERY BEGINNING, PEOPLE DIDN'T REALLY LIKE PORK BELLY ON THE MENU. IT WASN'T POPULAR JUST YET. SO I CAME UP WITH A NAME THAT SOUNDED MORE APPEALING. FIRST WE CALLED IT BACON STEAKIE. PEOPLE LOVE BACON AND MOST PEOPLE IN TEXAS LOVE STEAK, SO WE GAVE THEM WHAT THEY WANTED. ALL OF A SUDDEN, WE WERE SELLING MORE THAN 40 ORDERS A NIGHT. THEN PORK BELLY REALLY TOOK OFF. THE BACON SEN IS A DIFFERENT VERSION, IN WHICH THE PORK BELLY IS CURED WITH SUGAR AND SALT AND THEN ROASTED. IT'S SLICED AND PORTIONED AND THEN GRILLED TO ORDER BEFORE SERVING. THE FRIED APPLE PURÉE AND THE KIMCHEE APPLES ADD SPICE AND SWEETNESS.

**PORK BELLY**
6 ounces sugar
6 ounces salt
1 pound pork belly

**FISH CARAMEL**
(See page 59 for recipe.)

**CIPPOLINI ONIONS**
6 ounces cippolini onion
1 ounce vegetable oil
Kosher salt to taste
Fresh ground black pepper to taste

**SHAVED FENNEL**
1 bulb fennel
Ice water bath

**FRIED APPLE PURÉE**
(See page 60 for recipe.)

**GARNISH**
Fresh cilantro

**FOR THE PORK BELLY:** Preheat oven to 300° F. In a medium bowl, combine the sugar and salt and mix well. Cover the entire fat side of the pork belly with the sugar and salt mixture and place on a roasting rack in a roasting pan. (Be sure the pan has sides so that the runoff fat can be contained.) Bake the belly, fat side up, at 300° F until skin is a nice golden brown and caramelized, 30 to 45 minutes. The skin should be crispy to the touch. Remove from the oven and allow to rest at room temperature for about 15 minutes. Raise the temperature of the oven to 500° F. Brush the rested cooked pork belly with fish caramel and return to the oven to caramelize, 2 to 3 minutes. Remove from oven and cut to desired portion size.

**FOR THE CIPPOLINI ONIONS:** Peel the onions and cut them into ½-inch wedges. Place a small sauté pan over high heat and allow the pan heat up. Add the vegetable oil and let the oil heat up until just before the smoking point. Place the cut onions into the hot oil and let them caramelize on each side. Lower heat and continue to cook until onions are tender. Season to taste. Remove from pan when finished and serve immediately.

**FOR THE SHAVED FENNEL:** With a mandolin, shave fennel into paper-thin slices. Place shaved fennel into a container with ice water to shock and give it a more toothsome texture. Let the shaved fennel sit in ice bath for about 1 minute, and remove from ice water and let dry on a few paper towels. Use immediately.

**ASSEMBLY:** Place a large spoonful of apple purée onto the center of a plate. Drag your spoon through the purée to create a streaked effect. Place the pork belly on top of the purée and place the cooked onions around the pork belly. Top the pork belly with the shaved fennel and finish with fresh picked cilantro.

BACON SEN

# COBIA CRUDO
## *CARIBBEAN KINGFISH, CUCUMBER, JALAPEÑO*

THIS DISH HAS CUCUMBERS PREPARED IN THE TRADITIONAL JAPA-NESE METHOD OF PICKLING. YOU SLICE THE CUCUMBERS REALLY THIN ON A MANDOLIN, ADD A BUNCH OF SALT, AND LET THEM SIT OUT FOR ABOUT AN HOUR. THEN YOU PUT THEM ALL IN A BOWL AND SQUEEZE ALL OF THE LIQUID OUT OF THEM. THEY ALMOST LOOK LIKE THEY'RE SOMETHING FROM THE OCEAN. WE LINE THIS UP ON THE PLATE AND SLICE THE COBIA REALLY THIN AND PLACE THAT ON TOP. THIS DISH IS ALL ABOUT THE TEXTURES, FROM THE CUCUMBERS AND FISH TO THE CRUNCHY FRESH SERRANO PEPPERS.

**FOR THE PICKLED SHALLOT:** Peel and thinly slice the shallots and reserve in a bowl with the other vegetables. Combine water, sugar, vinegar, and salt in a small sauce pot over medium-high heat. Bring to the boiling point and remove from heat. Pour hot mixture over sliced vegetables and let cool to room temperature. Refrigerate and reserve for later use.

**FOR THE CURED CUCUMBER:** With a mandolin, slice the cucumber into $1/16$-inch discs. Place the sliced cucumbers into a stainless bowl and toss with the salt. Let the cucumbers sit in the refrigerator until the moisture begins to pull out, about 20 minutes. Remove the cucumbers from the bowl and remove excess moisture by using a towel to drain the water. Reserve cucumber for later use.

**FOR THE KAFFIR LIME OIL:** Peel and thinly slice shallots and garlic across the grain. Thinly slice lemongrass on the bias. Very thinly slice kaffir lime leaves. Slice Thai chile across the pepper, in very thin rounds. Heat a large sauté pan over medium heat. Place enough oil to coat the bottom of the pan and slowly heat. Place vegetables into the oil and sweat over medium heat to release the flavors. Season with salt and pepper. Once vegetables are translucent, add the remaining oil and let it heat through to combine and steep flavor. Remove from heat and let cool to room temperature. Reserve for later use.

**ASSEMBLY:** On a rectangular plate, place the cured cucumbers across the center, leaving an inch on either side. Place the sliced cobia across the cucumber. Place the jalapeño on the fish and finish with kaffir lime oil, yuzu juice, and pickled vegetables. Top with mint sprigs and serve immediately.

---

1½ ounces cobia, sliced thin

*PICKLED SHALLOT*

2 whole shallots

1 ounce fresh ginger, julienned

1 ounce negi, sliced thin

½ ounce myoga, sliced thin*

4 ounces water

2½ ounces sugar

1½ ounces white vinegar

kosher salt to taste

*Myoga is a Japanese ginger bud. It can be found in some Asian markets.*

*CURED CUCUMBER*

1 large English cucumber

¼ ounce salt

*KAFFIR LIME OIL*

3½ ounces shallots

4¼ ounces garlic

½ ounce lemongrass

⅛ ounce kaffir lime leaves

pinch of Thai chile

11½ ounces vegetable oil

Kosher salt to taste

Freshly ground black pepper

*GARNISH*

Sliced jalapeño

Yuzu juice

Mint sprigs

**MAINE MUSSELS**

2 pounds whole
    Maine mussels

4 ounces white wine

2 ounces white soy sauce

2 ounces onion,
    rough chopped

2 cloves garlic,
    rough chopped

3 ounces fresh basil

**BASIL BLOSSOM OIL**

1 clove garlic, peeled

½ shallot, peeled

7 ounces vegetable oil

Kosher salt to taste

½ ounce basil blossoms

**HEIRLOOM TOMATO
WATER**

(See page 62 for recipe.)

**INGREDIENTS
FOR ASSEMBLY**

Kosher salt and fresh
    ground black pepper
    to taste

2 ounces English
    cucumber, ¼-inch dice

2 heirloom tomatoes,
    chopped in 1-inch
    wedges and halved

Fresh basil leaves

Basil blossoms

# KAI JIRU
## *MAINE MUSSELS WITH TOMATO WATER AND BASIL*

WE PLAYED AROUND A LOT WITH MAKING DIFFERENT FLAVORED WATERS AT THE RESTAURANT. WE HAD MADE TOMATO WATER FOR SOME OTHER SPECIALS, AND WE TRIED IT OUT ON STEAMED MUSSELS. THE KEY TO THIS IS THAT THE TOMATO WATER HAS TO BE REALLY COLD. IT'S LIKE A BLOODY MARY ON CRACK. THE CILANTRO ADDS A NICE BITE, THE CELERY ADDS TEXTURE, AND THE TOMATO WATER HAS AMAZING FLAVOR. IT'S FANTASTIC.

**FOR THE MUSSELS:** Clean the mussels under cold water, removing any sediment and sand. Pull off the "beard" of the mussels. In a large lidded sauce pot, combine wine, white soy, onion, and garlic and bring to a boil. Add whole mussels and basil. Cover with a lid and steam to cook the mussels, 5 to 7 minutes. The mussels will open up completely when they have fully cooked. Remove them from the pot and place in refrigerator to cool off completely. Once the mussels have cooled, remove them from their shells and reserve in a stainless steel bowl.

**FOR THE BASIL BLOSSOM OIL:** Thinly slice garlic and shallots across the grain. Heat a large sauté pan over medium heat and place enough oil to coat the bottom of the pan. Place the vegetables into the heated oil and sweat over medium heat to release the flavors. You do not want any color on the vegetables. Add salt and the rest of the oil and let it heat through to combine and steep the flavors. Cool the oil and add the basil blossoms once the oil is at room temperature or cooler.

**ASSEMBLY:** Toss the chilled mussels in the stainless bowl with salt and pepper and ½ ounce of the basil blossom oil. Add the cucumber and tomatoes and toss to evenly coat all of the ingredients. In a deep, small chilled bowl, place the mussel and tomato mixture at the bottom and fill the bowl with 3 to 4 ounces heirloom tomato water. Garnish mussels and tomato water with a bit of the basil blossom oil, fresh torn basil leaves, and some basil blossoms. Serve immediately.

UCHI TIPS

**TOMATO WATER**

There a number of ways you can make tomato water, but the best way to get the most flavor is to take time, like 8 hours. We crush a lot of tomatoes, put them in a strainer and a fine filter, and leave it in the cooler overnight to drain. It takes a lot of tomatoes to make just a little bit of tomato water, but it's worth it for the end result. Tomato water is a component that really makes the Kai Jiru dish. It's perfect. And it also goes great with watermelon.

KOVICHE

# KOVICHE

## *SCALLOP, TOMATILLO, OLIVE, BLACK LIME*

THIS IS OUR VERSION OF CEVICHE. THIS IS A PERFECT EXAMPLE OF PAUL QUI'S TAKING A CHALLENGE THAT I WANTED TO ACHIEVE AND MAKING IT EVEN BETTER. IT'S THIN-SLICED TOMATILLO WITH THIN SLICES OF FRESH DIVER SCALLOP AND BLACK LIME SALT. THERE'S ALSO SOME OLIVE POWDER WITH IT. IT'S AN UNEXPECTED COMBINATION OF FLAVORS, BUT IT WORKS AMAZINGLY WELL.

2 diver scallops

*CURRY APPLE GASTRIQUE*

16 ounces apple juice

16 ounces white vinegar

½ ounce red curry

8 ounces sugar

*BLACK OLIVE POWDER*

7 ounces sugar

2 ounces dehydrated
    black olive*

3 ounces high-quality
    olive oil

10 ounces maltodextrin

*BLACK LIME SALT*

2 ounces dehydrated
    lime pulp**

¼ ounce maldon salt

*CORN FLAKE TUILE*

16 ounces milk

1 ounce butter

3 ounces sugar

¼ ounce salt

3 ounces cornflakes

*GARNISH*

1 tomatillo

A dash of olive oil

A squeeze of lime juice

A few sprigs of cilantro

**FOR THE CURRY APPLE GASTRIQUE:** Combine all ingredients in a medium saucepan, and reduce over medium heat until it reaches a syrup-like consistency.

**FOR THE BLACK OLIVE POWDER:** Place sugar into small saucepan and moisten with water. Heat the sugar until it caramelizes and remove from heat. Immediately pour the caramelized sugar onto a silicon baking mat and reserve until completely cooled. In a food processor grind the dehydrated olive and the cooled caramelized sugar to a fine crumb. Place the olive oil into a large separate bowl and slowly whisk in the maltodextrin until you have reached a powder-like consistency. Add the ground candied olives and reserve in an airtight container.

**FOR THE BLACK LIME SALT:** Combine the ingredients and store in an airtight container.

**FOR THE CORN FLAKE TUILE:** Preheat oven to 300° F. Heat milk, butter, sugar, and salt in a medium saucepan to a simmer. Add the corn flakes and continue to simmer for 5 minutes. Purée the mixture until smooth. While the mix is hot, pour on to a silicon baking mat-lined sheet tray, working quickly, before batter begins to set. Bake 25 to 30 minutes, rotating the sheet pan to ensure consistent cooking. Tuile should be a light, golden brown.

**ASSEMBLY:** Streak a rectangular plate with the curry apple gastrique. Slice the tomatillo into 1/8-inch slices and slice in half crosswise. Place 6 pieces across a rectangular plate, spaced evenly. Slice 2 scallops into 3 pieces each, cutting across the grain, and place on top of the tomatillos. Season the scallops with the black lime salt, a dash of olive oil, and lime juice. Place a 2-inch corn tuile across the top of each scallop. Finish with black olive powder and cilantro.

*\*Prepare the dehydrated olive the day before. Place in a dehydrator overnight, or in a gas oven with the pilot light on or an electric oven set to 100° F.*
*\*\*Prepare the dehydrated lime pulp the day before. Place about 4 ounces of fresh lime pulp in a dehydrator overnight, or in a gas oven with the pilot light on or an electric oven set to 100° F.*

**CITRUS**

I like the brightness and the refreshing quality of citrus. It goes so well with different types of fish. For me, it has evolved into a large part of my cuisine. It's a perfect acid that adds just the right balance to a dish. And it doesn't have to be complicated: Just a squeeze of a really good fresh lemon kicks up any dish, whether its sushi, a salad, whatever.

# MAME YAKI
## *SPICY GRILLED ENGLISH PEAS, KIMCHEE*

THIS IDEA COINCIDES WITH WHAT I WANTED FROM THE UCHI SALAD— SOMETHING YOU COULD EAT WITH YOUR HANDS. I WANTED TO HAVE SOMETHING DIFFERENT THAN THE TYPICAL EDAMAME. ONE DAY, WE PLAYED AROUND WITH SOME PEAS WE HAD AND GRILLED THEM WITH A SWEET CHILE SAUCE AND TOGARASHI (A JAPANESE 7-SPICE BLEND). THEY TURNED OUT TO BE THE PERFECT SNACK.

**ASSEMBLY:** Season and coat the peas, in pod, with oils, salt, and pepper, and place in a grill basket. Grill on the hot part of the grill to get a slight char. Flip the peas around to get the char on the whole pod. Remove the pea pods, and toss with the kimchee base in a large mixing bowl. Serve immediately.

4 ounces English peas

Drizzle of vegetable oil

Drizzle of chile oil

Kosher salt and fresh
  ground black pepper
  to taste

2 ounces kimchee base
  (See page 67 for recipe.)

# KAKI NO SHIKI
## *KUSSHI OYSTER WITH LYCHEE ICE*

WE'VE DONE OYSTERS MAYBE 500 DIFFERENT WAYS AT UCHI. THIS ONE IS REALLY GOOD BECAUSE I LIKE THE TEXTURE OF THE GRANITÉ, OR ICE. IT'S LIKE AN ASIAN-STYLE SNOW CONE. WE WANTED TO DO SOMETHING SUPER COLD WITH THE FROZEN GRANITÉ AND THEN ADD SOMETHING THAT WOULD BE SIMILAR TO TAPIOCA PEARLS IN BUBBLE TEA. THE SAKE FLAVOR GIVES IT A CRISP, CLEAN QUALITY.

4 kusshi oysters

*LYCHEE ICE*
8 ounces fresh lychee
½ ounce sugar
4 ounces water
Pinch kosher salt

*SAKE GELÉE*
2 sheets gelatin
ice water
4 ounces high-quality sake
4 ounces water
½ ounce sugar
Kosher salt to taste

**FOR THE KUSSHI OYSTERS:** Clean oysters by running them under a gentle stream of cold water, removing any sand or sediment. With an oyster knife, shuck oysters and disconnect from the shell. Reserve the oysters on ice.

**FOR THE LYCHEE ICE:** Remove fresh lychee from their outer skin and cut them in half to remove the pit. In a blender, combine the fruit, sugar, and water, and blend to a smooth juice-like consistency. Salt the mixture to taste. (It is not necessary to add too much salt as the oysters are naturally briny.) Place the juice into a flat container with high sides in freezer to freeze solid, at least 4 hours. Once the juice is fully frozen, use a fork to scrape the ice into snow cone-like consistency.

**FOR THE SAKE GELÉE:** Bloom gelatin in ice water until sheets are pliable, about 5 minutes. Squeeze out excess water and reserve gelatin. In a small saucepan, heat up sake with water and sugar over medium heat. Heat until sugar is completely dissolved. When mixture is heated, add bloomed gelatin and mix well to combine. Salt the mixture to taste and strain it through a fine mesh sieve. Pour strained liquid into a small flat container and refrigerate to set for at least 4 hours. When gelée has set, cut into desired shapes for use.

**ASSEMBLY:** Fill a shallow bowl with crushed ice and place 4 of the shucked oysters onto the ice. With a small spoon, place about a teaspoon of lychee ice onto the oyster in the half shell. Top the oyster and shaved ice with a small dice of the sake gelée. Serve immediately.

UCHI TIPS

**ICE**

I like to use ice because Japanese food is so temperature specific. Ice brings out the brightness of food. I tend to like everything cold, probably because we're in Texas where everything is hot. But it's so refreshing. And I think part of the draw of sushi is that it's so clean and crisp. For Uchi, I bought a really high-end snow cone machine to make crushed ice for serving sashimi, and it just makes the taste that much better.

UCHI, THE COOKBOOK

## POACHED LOBSTER

3 quarts water

1 ounce salt

1 16-ounce live
   whole lobster

Ice bath

## CANARY MELON
## GAZPACHO

1 large ripe canary melon,
   or seasonal melon such
   as honeydew

½ teaspoon kosher salt

½ ounce sugar

2 ounces water

## YELLOW BELL PEPPER
## PIPERADE

16 ounces yellow bell
   pepper, diced

6 ounces shallot, peeled
   and diced

3 ounces garlic, peeled
   and diced

Kosher salt

6 ounces olive oil

½ teaspoon paprika

Handful fresh flat leaf
   parsley, finely chopped

## CILANTRO PURÉE

2 garlic cloves

1 whole shallot

6 ounces vegetable oil

Salt

1 ounce cilantro leaves

Ice bath

## THAI CHILE OIL

1 shallot

3 garlic cloves

8 ounces vegetable oil

2 Thai chiles

Kosher salt to taste

## GARNISH

Fresh parsley

# OMARU EBI
## *POACHED LOBSTER WITH CANARY MELON GAZPACHO*

THIS STEMMED FROM MY DESIRE TO PRESENT LOBSTER IN THE BEST WAY POSSIBLE. LOBSTER IS SO EASY TO OVERCOOK. HERE, THE LOBSTER IS COOKED PERFECTLY AND THEN CHILLED. WARM LOBSTER IS BEST SERVED WITH WARM BUTTER, BUT I DON'T DO THE BUTTER THING. I PREFER TO KEEP IT CLEANER THAN THAT. SO THIS DISH IS ABOUT MY NEVER-ENDING FASCINATION WITH FRUIT. MELON WAS THE PERFECT COMPLEMENT TO THE COLD LOBSTER. ANY SEASONAL MELON WORKS, BUT HONEYDEW HAS THE BEST FLAVOR WITH THIS. IT'S ONE OF MY FAVORITE DISHES.

**FOR THE POACHED LOBSTER:** Bring the water and salt to a boil. Place the lobster in a high-sided stainless steel container. Set up a bath of iced water in a separate high-sided container, using plenty of ice. When the water reaches a boil, pour it over the live lobster and let the hot water cook the lobster. Let it poach for 9 minutes. Using a set of tongs, immediately place the poached lobster into an ice bath to stop the cooking process. Leave lobster in ice bath for 10 minutes to ensure it has fully cooled. With a kitchen towel and your hands, twist lobster where the tail meets the head to separate them. Use kitchen shears to cut the lobster tail lengthwise. Use your hands to gently remove the tail meat, keeping it intact. Remove the claw and knuckle from the head by twisting at the base of the arm, where it meets the head. Use shears to cut the knuckle shell in half to expose the meat, gently remove it, and reserve with the tail meat. Wrap the claw in a kitchen towel and use a soft mallet or the back end of a knife to crack the shell. Gently remove the claw meat, making sure the disc-shaped shell has been removed from the meat. Reserve all meat in the refrigerator. You can reserve the lobster shell and head for a stock or bisque for later use.

**FOR THE CANARY MELON GAZPACHO:** Pick the ripest melon you can find. The melon should be fragrant through the peel and have a hollow sound when you thump the top. Peel all of the skin from the meat of the melon and then split it in half vertically. With a large spoon, remove the seeds. Chop melon into small uniform pieces, about ½ inch in size. Place all ingredients into a blender and pulse to start the blending process. Purée until a uniform consistency is reached. Check taste and add more salt or sugar if necessary. It should have a naturally sweet taste from the ripeness of the melon. Reserve melon purée in refrigerator for later use.

**FOR THE YELLOW BELL PEPPER PIPERADE:** Sweat bell pepper, shallots, garlic, and salt in olive oil until tender. Add paprika and remove from heat. When mixture has cooled down, add chopped parsley. Reserve at room temperature for later use

**FOR THE CILANTRO PURÉE:** Peel and rough chop garlic and shallot to a uniform size. In a small sauté pan, gently sweat garlic and shallots in 1 ounce of the vegetable oil and a pinch of salt over low heat. While garlic and shallots are (continued on page 112 . . .)

To serve the best food possible, we rely on the freshest ingredients. A few years ago we devised a list of the flavor profiles and combinations we wanted to adhere to for the Uchi menu. It became a guide for us to maintain consistency with our food.

*(. . . Omaru Ebi continued)*

heating, bring a small sauce pot of salted water to a boil. Prepare an ice bath for shocking cilantro after it is blanched. Blanch cilantro leaves in boiling water for about 30 seconds, and then immediately shock in ice bath. Place on paper towels to soak up excess water. Place sweated shallot and garlic, with cooking oil, into a stainless bowl and place on ice bath to cool down. In a blender, purée remaining oil, cooked shallots/garlic, and blanched cilantro. Try to keep oil as cool as possible while blending to keep it from turning color. Once all ingredients are consistently puréed, remove from blender and cool down again on ice bath. Reserve cilantro purée at room temperature for later use.

**FOR THE THAI CHILE OIL:** Slice the shallot about 1/16 of an inch on the cross section. Brunoise garlic and combine with shallot in vegetable oil. Slice Thai chiles in rounds, seeds intact, as thinly as possible. Add chile rounds to oil and

gently heat on low flame. Once oil is fragrant, remove from heat and let steep to develop more flavor. Salt to taste and reserve at room temperature for later use.

**ASSEMBLY:** Cut the lobster tail into about 1-inch portions. You will get 4 portions from the 1-pound lobster. Fill 2/3 of a small bowl with the canary melon gazpacho. Toss the portioned lobster with the piperade to evenly coat the lobster meat. Divide the portioned lobster between the 4 bowls and place on top of the gazpacho. Spoon the cilantro purée around the lobster on top of the gazpacho, and finish the bowl with drops of Thai chile oil and fresh parsley.

FLAVOR PROFILES + COMBINATIONS — uchi Dec. 2006

Fruits, etc.

| Fruits, etc. | | JAPANESE | NO! | techniques |
|---|---|---|---|---|
| PEACHES | GOLD BEETS | WHITE SESAME | COCONUT | GELEES |
| PLUMS | DAIKON | BLACK SESAME | MANGO | BRAISES |
| NECTARINES | FENNEL | MIRIN | PINEAPPLE | ROASTED |
| CHERRIES | MAPLE | SOY | JALAPENO | BAKED |
| APPLES | CUCUMBER | SAKE | SOUR CREAM | STUFFED |
| GRAPES | HONEY | YUKARI | TRUFFLE OIL | INFUSIONS |
| PEARS | PISTACHIO | EDAMAME | NOODLES | REDUCTIONS |
| WATERMELON | CILANTRO | SEA SALT | BANANNAS | FROZEN |
| GRAPEFRUIT | LEEKS | KATSUOBUSHI | STAR FRUIT | ZEST |
| LYCHEE | KAFFIR LIME | RICE WINE VINEGAR | BOC CHOY | PICKLE |
| KUMQUATS | THYME | TOFU | OLIVES | SORBETS |
| PERSIMMONS | JASMINE | MISO | | GRILLED |
| FIGS | YELLOW BELLS | DAIKON | | STEAMED |
| RAW BERRIES | APRICOTS | MIOGA | | MARINADES |
| GINGER | CURRANTS | CHRYSTHMUM | | BRINES |
| MELON | SPEARMINT | WASABI | | CURES |
| ALMOND | LEMON THYME | GREEN TEA | | NIMONOS/SIMMERED |
| PEANUT | PEAS | BROWN RICE TEA | | CUSTARDS |
| SOY BEAN | JICAMA | NORI | | SOUPS |
| VANILLA | STILTON | SHISO | | GRATED |
| QUINCE | GOLD RAISINS | SANSHO | | SMASHED |
| LIME | MARCONA | YUZU | | SLICED |
| MEYER LEMON | ROSEMARY | MATSUTAKE | | KATSURA |
| HIBISCUS | PUMPKIN | SHIITAKE | | FRIED |
| BLUEBERRY | QUINOA | ENOKI | | SOUSVIDE |
| CINNAMON | PARSNIP | SHIMEJI | | ROLLED |
| LEMONGRASS | CHANTRELLE | TATSOI | | RAW |
| STAR ANISE | SPEARMINT | HOISIN | | MIXED |
| STRAWBERRY | WHITE ASPARAGUS | WHITE SOY | | EMULSIFIED |
| RAINIER CHERRIES | CONCORD GRAPES | DASHI | | BLENDED |
| PEPPERCORN | | UME | | OILS |
| TUMERIC | | PLUM WINE | | CANDIED |
| FISH SAUCE | | RICE | | SEARED |
| KIWI | | TARO | | |
| FUJI APPLE | | RENKON | | |
| FORELLE PEARS | | KANTON | | |
| DATES | | BURDOCK | | |
| POMEGRANATE | | MITSUBA | | |
| DRAGON FRUIT | | SHICHIMI | | |
| | | WAKAME | | |

# SHIKI SUZUKI
## *GRILLED LUBINA, TOMATO BROTH, GRILLED HEIRLOOM TOMATOES*

**THIS IS A SIMPLE FISH DISH WITH A BROTH THAT'S NOT A SOUP OR JUST A BORING SAUCE. THE LUBINA IS IN THE BASS FAMILY. IT'S VERY MILD. WE GRILLED THE TOMATOES AND THEN SERVED THEM IN A TOMATO-BASED SAUCE WITH BRANDY AND SHISO. IT'S LIGHT BUT HAS A RICH QUALITY TO IT.**

4 ounces lubina

Salt and pepper

**TOMATO BROTH**

3½ ounces vegetable oil

6 ounces shrimp shells

2 ounces lemongrass

3 Thai chiles

3 ounces garlic, sliced

9 ounces shallot, sliced

½ ounce salt

1 ounce fish sauce

4½ ounces brandy

34 ounces whole heirloom
   tomatoes

32 ounces water

**GRILLED HEIRLOOM
TOMATOES**

2 grilled heirloom tomatoes

Salt and pepper to taste

Drizzle of olive oil

**GARNISH**

Shiso leaves

**FOR THE TOMATO BROTH:** In a stock pot, heat the vegetable oil, add the shrimp shells, and cook until they are roasted and have turned from pink to slightly caramelized. Sauté the lemongrass, Thai chile, garlic, shallots, and salt over high heat, while stirring constantly. Cook until translucent. Deglaze the pan with ½ of the fish sauce to coat the contents of the pot. Add the brandy. When brandy has cooked out, add the whole tomatoes and water and let cook until the tomatoes have released all of their natural water. Lower heat and let the stock simmer until it coats the back of a spoon. Season with remaining fish sauce to taste, strain through a chinois, and reserve.

**FOR THE GRILLED HEIRLOOM TOMATOES:** Season and oil 2 heirloom tomatoes with salt, pepper, and olive oil, and grill the whole tomatoes until cooked through.

**FOR THE GRILLED LUBINA:** Season the fillet with salt and pepper, and grill skin side down until skin begins to caramelize and crisp. Finish cooking the fish through on the other side of the fillet. Remove the fish from grill and let rest.

**ASSEMBLY:** In a large bowl, place the broth down first. Follow with the grilled fish fillet and place the grilled tomatoes next to the fish. Finish the plate with torn shiso leaves, and serve immediately.

UCHI TIPS

**FINDING FISH**

We use a variety of fish from all over the world. Some of it may be difficult to find where you live. The best advice is to develop a good relationship with the best supermarket in your city. Most of those places can order fish for you if they don't already have it. If you can buy it whole, that maintains the best integrity, but if it's a larger fish, they can butcher it for you fresh. A special order is always better than ordering it straight from the case, because then you know when it came in and how fresh it is.

# TAKE NABE *MUSHROOM BOWL*

**THIS IS ENTIRELY A PAUL QUI DISH. IT REMINDS ME OF CONGEE, WHICH IS ESSENTIALLY AN ASIAN RISOTTO. THIS DEFINITELY FALLS WITHIN THE REALM OF "COMFORT FOOD" FOR US. IT'S ALMOST LIKE A RICE PORRIDGE. THE GOAL WAS TO TAKE ADVANTAGE OF THE FLAVOR OF THE MUSHROOMS. WE SERVE IT WITH THE RICE AND THE DASHI STOCK IN A HOT POT WITH BONITO FLAKES. IT ALL STEAMS TOGETHER, AND IT'S JUST AMAZING.**

**BONITO FLAKES**

In Japanese, these are called katsuobushi. Katsuo is a jackfish that is usually caught around Japan in the fall. In Japan, they take this fish and dry it. It gets to where a fillet almost looks like petrified wood. Then they take that and shave it into small flakes. It's one of the 3 or 4 core ingredients for traditional Japanese food. It's what you use to make dashi, which is used in just about any broth made in Japan.

**DASHI BROTH**

2 ounces sake

1 ounce white soy sauce

2 ounces water

1 ounce soy sauce

1 ounce mirin

**TAKE NABE**

½ ounce butter

3½ ounces cooked rice

3 ounces dashi broth
  (See recipe above.)

1 ounce enoki mushrooms

1 ounce honjemiji mushroom

½ ounce negi rounds

1 egg yolk

Pinch of bonito flakes

Juice and zest of 1 lemon

A few mitsuba leaves

**FOR THE DASHI BROTH:** In a small sauce pot, heat the sake to the boiling point, when sake flames. Continue to cook until all alcohol has been cooked out, combine the remaining ingredients, and reserve in refrigerator.

**ASSEMBLY:** Heat the nabe, or Japanese hot pot, on the stove with the butter, and add the rice. Pour dashi broth over rice and add mushrooms and negi, cover with nabe lid, return to heat and let cook for 10 minutes. Top with egg and bonito flakes, return to stove, and cover to let the egg steam. Finish with lemon juice, lemon zest, and mitsuba leaves. Serve immediately.

TAI SHIO

1 whole bream

*KUMQUAT AND*
*GREEN PEPPERCORN*
Pinch ground green
    peppercorn
Pinch kosher salt
3½ ounces kumquats

*SALT CRUST FOR BREAM*
25 ounces kosher salt
¼ ounce yuzu juice
5 ounces water

*TOMATO VINAIGRETTE*
9 ounces heirloom
    tomatoes
1 ounce sherry vinegar
2 ounces olive oil
Salt and pepper to taste

*KAFFIR LIME OIL*
8 ounces peeled shallots
10 Kaffir lime leaves
8 ounces soybean oil,
    enough to cover the
    bottom of a pan

# TAI SHIO
## *SALT-BAKED BREAM, CALAMANSI, TOMATO, KAFFIR LIME*

THIS IS A WHOLE FISH WITH SALT CRUST. BREAM IS PROBABLY ONE OF MY FAVORITE FISH OTHER THAN SNAPPER. THE SALT CRUST STEAMS IT IN THE OVEN. THEN WE PULL IT OUT OF THE CRUST AND SERVE IT WITH SOME KAFFIR LIME. IT'S A GREAT BALANCED DISH.

**FOR THE KUMQUAT AND GREEN PEPPERCORN:** Combine the green peppercorn and salt. Thinly slice the kumquats and lightly season with the ground green peppercorn salt. Reserve for later use.

**FOR THE SALT CRUST AND BREAM:** Preheat your oven to 450° F. Combine all ingredients and mix well. Place a layer of the salt down on a sheet tray. Place the whole bream on top and completely cover with the salt mix. With your finger, form a groove all the way around the crusted fish, so the salt shell will be easier to break off when finished baking. Bake for 25 minutes on a parchment-lined baking pan. Once finished, remove the fish from the oven and let rest for 5 minutes. Separate the salt crust to remove the fish.

**FOR THE TOMATO VINAIGRETTE:** With a microplane or zester, grate the tomatoes and remove the large pieces of tomato skins. Next add the sherry, and slowly whisk in the olive oil to emulsify. Season with salt and pepper to taste.

**FOR THE KAFFIR LIME OIL:** Using a mandolin or a sharp knife, slice the shallots into very thin rounds. Julienne the kaffir lime leaves and sweat both in soybean oil in a medium pan over medium heat until they become aromatic and the shallots are just translucent. Cool and reserve for later use.

**ASSEMBLY:** Place a sasapa leaf down on a large oblong plate and place the fish on top, perpendicular to the plate. In three separate containers place the kumquat seasoned with green peppercorn salt, the tomato vinaigrette, and the kaffir lime oil.

# UCHI SALAD
## *BABY ROMAINE SALAD WITH EDAMAME AND JALAPEÑO DRESSING*

THIS WAS A CHALLENGE I POSED TO PAUL QUI. I WANTED SOMETHING INTERACTIVE ON THE TABLE FOR THE CUSTOMER IN MUCH THE SAME WAY CHIPS AND SALSA ARE AT A TEX-MEX RESTAURANT. SO I ASKED FOR SOMETHING LIKE A SALAD THAT WAS CLEAN AND HEALTHY BUT THAT YOU COULD EAT WITH YOUR HANDS. WE CAME UP WITH THIS SAUCE, WITH ROASTED JALAPEÑOS AND EDAMAME, AND HYDROPONIC ROMAINE THAT WE GET FROM A LOCAL FARM CALLED BLUEBONNET FARMS.

*FOR THE EDAMAME-JALEPEÑO DRESSING:* Preheat oven to 450° F. Combine edamame, garlic, shallots, and vegetable oil over medium-high heat in a large skillet. Sweat the mix until ingredients become translucent. Strain and reserve oil. Place 2 or 3 whole jalapeños on a baking sheet and roast in the oven for 15 to 20 minutes. Let jalapeños cool, then peel and seed. Place vegetables in a blender along with the remaining raw jalapeños (seeds included). Start with a small amount of water, and purée, slowly adding more water. Add sushi zu. Emulsify by slowly adding the reserved oil while blending. Consistency should be about the same viscosity of mayonnaise.

*FOR THE BELL PEPPER PIPERADE:* Combine first 5 ingredients and sweat vegetables until tender. Add paprika and remove from heat. When mixture has cooled down, add chopped parsley. Reserve at room temperature for later use.

*ASSEMBLY:* Rinse and towel dry whole lettuce leaves. Place lettuce leaves, stem down, into two shot glasses, creating a bouquet-like arrangement in each glass. Add a small squeeze of lemon juice, a drizzle of olive oil, and a pinch of salt on the leaves. In another small vessel or cup, partially fill with edamame-jalapeño dressing. Spoon a small amount of the room-temperature piperade on top of dressing to finish.

*EDAMAME-JALAPEÑO DRESSING*

9 ounces edamame, shucked

2½ ounces peeled garlic, rough chopped

1½ ounces peeled shallots, rough chopped

2 to 4 ounces vegetable oil (as needed)

2½ ounces jalapeño

1 ounce sushi zu (See page 79 for recipe.)

2 ounces water (as needed)

*YELLOW BELL PEPPER PIPERADE*

6½ ounces yellow bell pepper, rough chopped

3½ ounces peeled shallot, rough chopped

1½ ounces peeled garlic, rough chopped

3½ ounces olive oil

Pinch kosher salt

Pinch paprika

Pinch finely chopped parsley

*SALAD*

1 head baby romaine lettuce

Fresh lemon juice, extra virgin olive oil, and salt to taste

# WAGYU MOMO
## *WAGYU SHORT RIBS, PEACH KIMCHEE, GARLIC CHIPS*

THE KIMCHEE PEACHES IN THIS DISH ARE MAYBE ONE OF THE TOP THREE SAUCES THAT PAUL QUI HAS EVER MADE. IT'S VERY SIMPLE. MARRY PEACHES WITH FRESHLY PREPARED KIMCHEE, AND THEN PURÉE THEM. IT'S SPICY AND SWEET. AND PAIRED WITH THE SHORT RIB, IT'S JUST A HOME RUN, A PRIME EXAMPLE OF WHAT UCHI FOOD IS. IT'S NOT JUST SHORT RIBS, WHICH IS SOMETHING EVERYBODY LOVES. IT'S SHORT RIBS PAIRED WITH UNEXPECTED FLAVORS THAT MAKE IT EVEN MORE INCREDIBLE.

*GARLIC CHIPS*

2 heads garlic

2 pots boiling water

24 ounces sugar

8 ounces water

Canola oil, enough to
   coat a frying pan with
   ¼ inch of oil

*WAGYU MOMO*

4 ounces Wagyu short ribs,
   sliced into 7 to 8 pieces

Salt and fresh ground
   pepper

1 ounce tamari for basting

2 ounces brown butter
   for basting

*PEACH KIMCHEE EMULSION*

(See page 71 for recipe.)

*GARNISH*

Fresh heirloom peach

Cilantro

***FOR THE GARLIC CHIPS:*** Peel whole cloves of garlic. Slice garlic paper thin on a mandolin or with a very sharp knife. Quickly blanch sliced garlic in a pot of boiling water for no more than 30 seconds. Remove garlic from boiling water and repeat step in the second pot of boiling water. Bring sugar and water to a boil in separate pot. Place blanched garlic into boiling mixture. Let garlic chips cook at a simmer for about 10 minutes or until translucent. In a frying pan, heat oil to 325° F and reserve at that temperature for frying. Remove garlic from syrup, rinse, and shake off excess water. Fry in heated oil until light golden brown. Reserve in an airtight container for use as a garnish.

***ASSEMBLY:*** Prepare a very hot gas or charcoal grill. Season the wagyu portions with salt and pepper and place over the hottest part of the grill. Sear on one side and flip. Glaze each side of the meat with the tamari. Cook to a rare/medium-rare, temperature basting the meat with brown butter regularly. Remove from grill and let rest for 3 or 4 minutes. Slice the beef against the grain into 7 to 8 pieces. Slice half of an heirloom peach into 7 to 8 slices. Place a smear of the peach kimchee emulsion in the middle of a square plate, place the beef onto the smear, and top with the sliced peaches. Finish the plate with garlic chips and fresh cilantro.

USAGI TAMAGO

# USAGI TAMAGO
## *RABBIT TERRINE, PEAR MOSTARDA, PICKLED QUAIL EGG*

THIS IS NOT SOMETHING YOU'D EXPECT TO SEE ON A SUSHI MENU, BUT IT'S A FANTASTIC DISH—ESPECIALLY WITH THE USE OF THE PICKLED QUAIL EGG IN THE CENTER. WE ROAST A WHOLE RABBIT AND MAKE A CONFIT, AND WE PULL THE MEAT AND HOLD IT IN OIL FOR A LITTLE WHILE AND THEN MAKE A TERRINE WITH A QUAIL EGG INSIDE. WE FINISH IT ON THE GRILL OR FLAT TOP FOR A NICE SEAR. THE PEAR MOSTARDA IS A GREAT CONTRAST FOR IT.

### RABBIT CURE

1 ounce juniper

1 ounce green peppercorn

1 ounce thyme

2 cinnamon sticks

12 ounces sugar

8 ounces salt

### RABBIT

1 rabbit

3 pounds butter, browned
(Cook the butter until solids begin to brown, and remove from heat.)

1 bunch fresh thyme

2 heads garlic

2 shallots, halved

1 tablespoon transglutaminase*

A few sprigs pea shoots for garnish

*Transglutaminase is a bonding agent for meat. It can be found online.*

### PEAR MOSTARDA

1 Asian pear

8 ounces white wine

4 ounces sugar

4 ounces mustard seeds

1 teaspoon rapid set pectin

### PICKLED QUAIL EGGS

(See page 70 for recipe.)

### FISH CARAMEL

(See page 59 for recipe.)

### ENGLISH PEA PURÉE

(See page 59 for recipe.)

**FOR THE RABBIT CURE:** Grind all spices and mix together with sugar and salt. Liberally coat rabbit with the cure mixture. Place on a baking tray and wrap the whole tray with plastic wrap. Refrigerate and let cure for 6 hours.

**COOKING METHOD FOR RABBIT:** Preheat oven to 350° F. Clean off excess cure from rabbit and place rabbit into a roasting pan. Cover rabbit with brown butter. Add thyme, garlic, and shallots. Wrap entire pan with foil and cook in oven for 4 hours, or until the meat falls off the bone. Let the rabbit rest in the roasting pan until it reaches room temperature.

**FOR THE PEAR MOSTARDA:** Peel and small dice the Asian pear. Simmer the pear in white wine and sugar in small sauce pot. In a pot of boiling salted water, blanch the mustard seeds twice to decrease intensity of flavor. Add blanched mustard seeds to the pear mixture. Add the rapid set pectin and cook on medium-low heat, while gently mixing until the mostarda thickens.

**METHOD FOR ASSEMBLY OF TERRINE:** Once the rabbit is cool enough to handle, pull all the meat off of the bones. Dust the rabbit meat and quail eggs with transglutaminase. Line a terrine mold with plastic wrap. Use enough to allow excess plastic to hang over sides of the mold.

Layer the rabbit meat halfway up the terrine mold. Place quail eggs on top of the first half of layered rabbit meat and continue to layer meat on top of eggs while carefully keeping them centered. Use remaining plastic wrap to seal terrine and press with a medium weight overnight.

**ASSEMBLY:** Cut a slice off the pressed and set terrine. Slice should be about 1 inch deep. Season lightly with salt and pepper and place on medium heat grill. Baste the terrine with fish caramel while grilling. To serve, place the pea purée on the plate. Put the hot, grilled terrine above the purée. Put a large spoonful of pear mostarda on top of the terrine. Garnish plate with pea shoots. Serve immediately.

1½ ounces hiramasa

**CURRY APPLE GASTRIQUE**

8 ounces apple juice

8 ouces white vinegar

⅛ ounce red curry

4 ounces sugar

**KIMCHEE OIL**

4 cloves garlic

1 shallot

½ inch piece of ginger

1 bunch of green onion

½ ounce Korean
      pepper flake

8 ounces vegetable oil

Salt and pepper

**APPLE CHIPS**

1 green apple

1 teaspoon simple syrup

*NOTE: Make this one day
      in advance.*

**FENNEL CHIPS**

1 bulb fennel

2 teaspoons simple syrup

*NOTE: Make this one day
      in advance.*

**GARNISH**

Green apple slices

Shaved fennel bulb

Fennel frond

Kosher salt

Juice of ½ lemon

# YELLOWTAIL RINGO
## *AMBERJACK, GREEN APPLE, FENNEL*

THE IDEA BEHIND THIS DISH WAS TO TAKE THE CONCEPT OF SASHIMI AND STAND IT ON ITS HEAD. INSTEAD OF ONE YAKUMI TO COMPLEMENT IT AS IN TRADITIONAL JAPANESE SUSHI, WE ADD THREE: APPLES, BOTH FRESH AND DEHYDRATED; A RED CURRY GASTRIQUE; AND FENNEL THREE WAYS, AS POLLEN, DEHYDRATED, AND FRESH. IT'S A SPICY, SWEET, AND FRUITY COMBINATION THAT WE SERVE WITH THINLY SLICED AMBERJACK ON A SCREAMING COLD PLATE.

**FOR THE CURRY APPLE GASTRIQUE:** Combine all ingredients in a medium sauce pot and reduce over medium heat until syrup-like consistency.

**FOR THE KIMCHEE OIL:** Peel garlic cloves and shallots and cut into ⅛-inch slices, crosswise. Peel the ginger and grate it on a microplane. Slice the green onion on a bias into ¼-inch pieces. In a large container that has a lid, combine the manicured garlic, shallot, ginger, and green onion with Korean pepper flakes and oil. Season with salt and fresh cracked pepper.

**FOR THE APPLE CHIPS:** With a mandolin, slice the apples paper thin. Coat the apples with simple syrup and lay side by side on a dehydrator tray. Place in a dehydrator overnight or in a gas oven with the pilot light on or an electric oven set to 100° F.

**FOR THE FENNEL CHIPS:** With a mandolin, slice the fennel paper thin. Coat the fennel with simple syrup and lay side by side on a dehydrator tray. Place in a dehydrator overnight or in a gas oven with the pilot light on or an electric oven set to 100° F.

**ASSEMBLY:** Season and sear the hiramasa on one side of the fish; slice 8 pieces of the hiramasa close to ¼ inch thick. Cut the fresh apple into ¼-inch slices, shave the fennel on a mandolin, and reserve for salad. Lay a spoonful of the gastrique down on a rectangular plate. Place the portioned fish on top of the gastrique. In a small bowl, make a salad of the fresh apple slices, shaved fennel, and fennel frond. Toss with kosher salt, lemon juice, and kimchee oil. Place this on top of the portioned fish. Finish the dish with apple chips and fennel chips. Garnish with fennel frond.

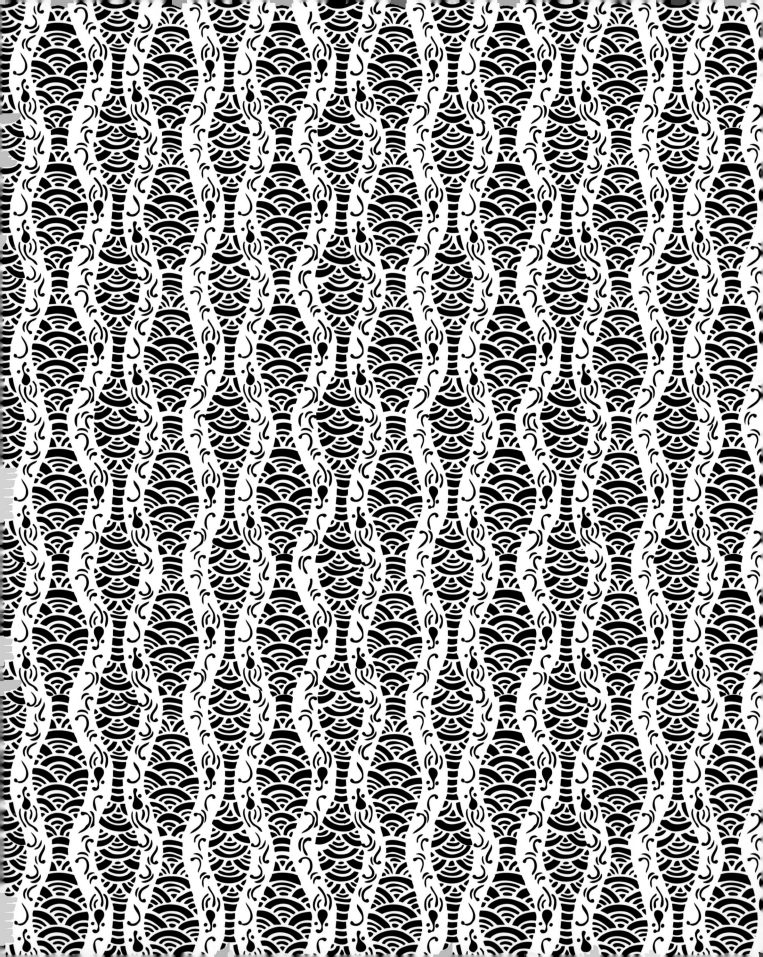

# SUSHI AND ROLLS

# BY THE BITE

A lot of people don't realize it, but sushi really means "vinegar rice." ("Su" means vinegar, "Shi" means rice.) It doesn't mean "fish" at all. To me, sushi is about having the perfect bite.

The best bite of sushi you can have is when it's made fresh, it's handed to you by the sushi chef, and you eat it on the spot. The rice should be warm and the fish should be cold. Keep in mind, the longer you let that piece sit, that perfect combination switches. If you allow it to sit long enough for the fish to become warm and the rice to become cold, then you've missed your window for a great piece of sushi.

The goal of a good sushi chef is to create that perfect bite just for you. The chef is essentially making your dinner one bite at a time for you to enjoy. There really is no greater delicacy.

That's where my food came from. When I had people at my counter, I was always trying to make things just a little bit better. How do you do that? You use techniques, quality ingredients, and the sharpest knives, and you treat your product as well as you can. That's the very least a good sushi chef should do. I like to push the boundaries just a little bit, with different flavor combinations and textures, to make what should be the perfect bite of sushi even better.

At Uchi, we've kept things simple by having only 10 rolls on the sushi menu. The reason is for consistency, to make the best possible rolls we can every time. I don't like it when I see other sushi restaurants offering a long list of sushi rolls. It's just silly at a certain point, and it inevitably means that the quality suffers. I have a mantra about moderation: Too much of anything is not good.

## UCHI TIPS

### NORI

Nori is the seaweed paper used in sushi rolls. At first, nori was a very off-putting taste for me, as it is for a lot of Americans. It's kind of "ocean-y." What people don't always realize is that there are different qualities of nori that you can buy. It is categorized by color. Gold nori is the best—it's what we use at Uchi. It's really firm and crunchy and salty. There's silver, bronze, blue, and yellow. Quality nori is more expensive, but the lower in price you go, you'll find that it's rubbery and tough. Nori is one of those key components that can help you make great sushi. It's all about the quality of your ingredients: the fish, the rice, and the nori.

## RECIPE NOTE

The sushi rolls recipes are designed for a single plating rather than designated to serve a certain quantity (i.e. Serves 6) for the same reason as our Daily Specials and Tastings. At Uchi, everything is meant to be shared. The individual sushi recipes are designed for a single serving.

# SUSHI 101

In my experience as a sushi chef, I've found that the average person doesn't really know what to do with this cuisine. So much of American cuisine is about big portions and piling on the add-ons. You get hot dogs and pizza with "the works" and hamburgers "all the way." That doesn't work for sushi. At Uchi, one of my primary goals was to take the sushi bar experience and bring it into the whole restaurant. I've trained my staff to pick up on what the customers like and dislike and guide them through a more educational and interactive experience. I want people leaving Uchi to have tried things they never would have expected ... and to have barely touched their soy sauce dish. Below are a few brutally honest tips worth knowing about enjoying sushi.

### SOY SAUCE

*You don't need to fill your soy dish to the brim.* It's not like someone is going to cheat you out of the soy sauce. There is more in the bottle, people.

*Don't put your sushi in the soy sauce.* You don't sit rice in soy sauce, if you even use soy sauce. You should wipe only a small amount of soy sauce on the fish, not the rice.

*Try to use as little soy sauce as possible.* Especially if the restaurant serves your sushi with other yakumi, or accents, that are meant to go with your order. The Japanese never serve soy sauce with sushi. You have to ask for it. There's a reason for that.

### WASABI

You're not supposed to make a paste, mortar, putty, or anything gloppy with wasabi and soy sauce. I've seen so many people take their wasabi "paste" and spread it on their sushi like they're buttering toast. Then they line up the pickled ginger on top like roof shingles. You can't even see the fish! And when they eat it and the wasabi knocks their eyes back into their head, they pat themselves on the back like they've achieved some rite of passage. And then they say, "This is the best sushi, ever." The truth is, they haven't even tasted the sushi!

### PICKLED GINGER

This is used to cleanse your palate. It's *not* to eat with your sushi. Not only is it pickled, but it's ginger. Two really strong flavors. So when people put that on their sushi, you know what they taste? PICKLED GINGER! Save the ginger for between bites. Do not eat it with your fish.

### DON'T ORDER ALL YOUR SUSHI AT ONCE

It makes you look like an asshole. Sushi is a delicacy. You're supposed to eat it one bite at a time right when it's made. I hate that long paper list most sushi restaurants have. It makes people think they have to order everything right then and there. When you place a large order, the chef makes all of it at once, which takes time, which makes the first piece old by the time they've finished the final piece. Then, when it gets to your table, it sits even longer as you work your way through it. If you want mediocre or bad sushi, order it that way. If you want good sushi, don't order it all at once.

### EAT YOUR SUSHI IMMEDIATELY WHEN YOU GET IT

With fresh French fries, you have only a few minutes to eat them before they're soggy and gross. Same with sushi. It's supposed to be cold fish and warm rice. Eat it when it's served. Otherwise it's just dying on your plate.

### DON'T ASK FOR THINGS THAT AREN'T ON THE MENU

People seem to think every restaurant has the same sushi. You don't see Big Macs at Burger King. You find them only at McDonald's. People need to respect the establishment they come into. If we don't have a rainbow roll, don't ask for it. Order what you see on the menu. There are people who get so mad when we tell them, "We don't have a rainbow roll. You have to go somewhere else to get that." But, I'm sorry, that's just not what we serve.

### A WORD ON CHOPSTICKS

You don't need them as much as you think you do. Sushi was originally made to eat with your hands. The only time you need chopsticks is for sashimi. Everything else, you can eat with your hands. Even nigiri, which is a piece of fish served on a small pod of rice.

### ONE BITE NIGIRI

Nigiri is the sushi rice pressed together with a slice of fish on top. You really shouldn't take two bites. It's supposed to be one bite. Unfortunately, some restaurants get carried away with the size of their nigiri. If it's just too big, hold it with your fingers. Smear a dab of soy sauce on top of the fish (not the rice) and take a bite. Then take the second bite without setting it down.

### CHEAP SUSHI IS AN OXYMORON

Half-price appetizer sushi ... cheap sushi ... that's a bad idea. Sushi should not be used to save money. It means you're eating bad fish. Period.

### AVOID THE SPICY TUNA ROLL

The two most popular sushi rolls in America are the California roll and the spicy tuna roll. California because it's delicious. It's the perfect combination of cucumber for texture, avocado for creaminess and a little fat, and crab for sweetness. California rolls are great. On the other hand, spicy tuna rolls come from sushi chefs in America trying to get rid of their older tuna with spicy mayonnaise. I would eat 1,001 things at a sushi bar other than a spicy tuna roll—unless it's at a really good restauraunt.

### RESPECT YOUR SUSHI CHEFS

The good ones really know what they're doing. If you have a chance to eat sushi, always do it at the sushi bar. Every sushi chef has a stash that they want to share. Just trust they're going to give you something good.

### BIGGER IS NOT BETTER

Sushi is supposed to be bite-size, and the rice is supposed to fall apart in your mouth. It's supposed to be small, simple, and clean, not overloaded with rice and a bunch of other stuff.

## DON'T BE HIGH MAINTENANCE

It's okay to ask for the occasional substitution. But when it comes to taste, the customer is not always right. Some substitutions are simple and that's fine, like a California roll with no crab. Fine. But if you come to Uchi and ask for hamachi belly, cut extra thin, with no skin, on small rice balls, with a slice of lemon on top and spicy sauce on the side, the answer will be "No."

## FRIED THINGS AREN'T SUSHI

It's amazing how people come in and order the unhealthiest things on the menu, like tempura-fried brie for an appetizer and tempura-fried sushi rolls, and then brag about how healthy their meal was. Uchi offers some of those things because it's what Americans want. But in general, don't order fried things if you're trying to enjoy the healthfulness of sushi.

## SUSHI RICE

It's supposed to be warm and it's supposed to be soft. It's not supposed to be sticky, hard, or crunchy. Sushi has everything to do with the rice, not the fish. You read food blogs that don't know what they're talking about, saying they had sushi fall apart on them (probably because they soaked it in soy sauce) and that the rice was too soft. Would you rather the rice be super sticky so it can absorb a lake of soy sauce and still maintain some structure? Gross. That's not how it's supposed to be.

## CLEAN YOUR PLATE

If you're in Japan or in a real Japanese restaurant, don't ever, ever, ever leave anything on your plate. You eat everything. Their philosophy is, "We're an island nation. We barely have enough resources. So when you have something on your plate, you had better be thankful for it. And you had better eat it."

## AVOID PRESLICED SUSHI

If you go to a sushi bar and everything is presliced, it's not a good sushi bar. You see presliced sushi at a lot of restaurants. It means it's cheap. It means the restaurant is cutting corners. They're not paying attention to the product or respect to the fish. They're exposing the fish to more air, which is breaking it down and ruining its texture.

## COLORFUL FISH DOES NOT ALWAYS EQUAL FRESH FISH

Ever seen someone take a look at a block of bright red tuna in a sushi case and say, "Man, that tuna looks so fresh!" There are five kinds of fish that Americans typically consume for sushi: tuna, salmon, yellowtail, eel, and a whitefish. You can buy any of those fish in a precut, preformed, preweighed block. You'll notice the tuna is really red, and the salmon is really orange. That's from the nitrates used to package the fish. Many sushi restaurants order that way because the fish is cheap and they don't need skilled labor to make their sushi. Bottom line: If it doesn't look natural, it probably isn't.

## WHAT TO KNOW ABOUT MACKEREL (SABA)

This is the number 1 type of sushi fish that is known for food poisoning. Saba is a very oily and particularly strong-tasting fish. It's the cheapest fish you can buy, and most restaurants cure it with salt so they can hold it for a long time. Some restaurants hold it for up to a week or ten days. That is where the food poisoning comes in. Some people really like saba, but if you don't trust the sushi restaurant, it's not smart to order this stuff. *Note: At Uchi, we buy all of our mackerel fresh and cure it in-house each day. Whatever is not used that day is then moved to our grilled mackerel dish, Saba Shio. After that, whatever is not used is discarded.*

## BEWARE OF TOO MUCH ESCOLAR

Not many people know this, but escolar is a natural laxative. It's a great fish to use for sushi, but order it only in small amounts. There are some big horror stories attached to it and those who have consumed too much of it.

## SAKE

It is meant to be enjoyed when it's very fresh and cold. It's amazing how well it goes with sushi. It's so clean and delicate. A lot of people don't know how to enjoy sake. They'll order a bottle of hot sake and sip on that for their whole meal. It's disgusting. In Japan, the only time they drink warm sake is at festivals when it's cold outside, sort of like how we drink mulled wine at holiday festivals. You wouldn't drink that stuff on a regular basis, though, especially because it's made from cheap wine. Guess what? Warm sake is also cheap. If you're going to pair your sake with sushi, be sure to order cold sake. Don't mess with the warm stuff.

## GOOD TUNA

What a lot of people don't realize is really good tuna, like bluefin, is actually better a few days after it's been caught. Just like beef goes through an aging process before it's considered good, tuna also has to go through a process of rigor mortis and loosening up before it has quality flavor. So technically, tuna is a kind of fish that's best when it's three to four days old, whereas a whitefish like snapper, which is leaner, needs to be eaten as soon as possible.

## JAPANESE KNIVES

These are the most fantastic knives. They're crafted of iron. Just like swords. The process of making one of these knives is so meticulous. They're also the sharpest knives, and they have single-edged blades. So one edge is flat and one edge is beveled. Geometrically, it's a more finite point as opposed to a double-edged blade where there are two angles coming together. When you slice with a single-edged blade, there's no friction at all.

## INTEGRITY OF FOOD

(One of my pet peeves) When you're cooking at home, the real secret to it all is maintaining the integrity of each ingredient. A great meal is well thought-out ahead of time, but that starts with the idea of paying attention to the integrity of each ingredient—when you're prepping it, when you're cooking it, when you're serving it. When someone puts something in their mouth, everything you've done up until that point has to be done with the best care and intention. Everything is supposed to be finitely specific. That's what defined Uchi food from the beginning, paying attention to the integrity of the ingredients.

# BOND ROLL

I LIVED IN NEW YORK FOR A LITTLE WHILE AND WORKED AT A RESTAURANT CALLED BOND STREET, WHICH IS WHAT I NAMED THIS ROLL AFTER. BOND STREET HAD A ROLL THAT HAD SUN-DRIED TOMATO IN IT, AND I WANTED TO DO SOMETHING SIMILAR. I THOUGHT THE COMBINATION OF THE SUN-DRIED TOMATO WITH AVOCADO WAS PERFECT, AND USING THE SOY PAPER INSTEAD OF NORI MAKES IT MORE USER-FRIENDLY FOR THE AMERICAN PALATE.

*BOND ROLL*

½ avocado

1 ounce sushi-grade
    salmon fillet

1 sun-dried tomato

½ sheet soy paper

3½ ounces sushi rice

*BOND SAUCE*

2 ounces sake

2 ounces mirin

2 ounces sugar

6 ounces miso

2 ounces yuzu juice

1 bunch shiso

*GARNISH*

Radish sprouts

**FOR THE BOND ROLL:** Quarter avocado lengthwise, peel the avocado and remove the pit. With a sharp knife, slice avocado into ⅛-inch slices, wrap with plastic wrap, and reserve in refrigerator until needed. Slice the salmon against the grain, into small slices. Julienne the sun-dried tomato and reserve. Lay the shiny side of the soy paper down and the length (the longer side) toward you. Using damp fingers, apply the sushi rice to cover the soy paper lengthwise. Leave about ½ inch of open strip on the top of the soy paper. Place the rice-lined soy sheet onto a sushi mat lined with plastic wrap with the rice side up (facing you). Place sliced avocado in the middle, end to end. Place the sliced salmon on top of the avocado in a line from end to end. Spread the sun-dried tomato on top of the ingredients, being sure to get a consistent line on the ingredients. Using the sushi mat as a guide, roll the rice-lined soy paper sheet up, while pressing and gently squeezing the mat in toward you to shape the roll. Continue the process until the sushi roll is a uniform cylinder with a tight roll. With a sharp knife, slice the roll into 8 pieces. To make cutting easier and cleaner, dip the blade into cold water before slicing.

**FOR THE BOND SAUCE:** Heat sake in a small sauce pot to burn off alcohol, a few minutes. Add mirin and heat to just below boiling point. Remove from heat and add sugar. Mix well to dissolve. Add miso and yuzu juice, and mix well to combine. Mince shiso and fold into all mixed ingredients. Refrigerate for later use.

**ASSEMBLY:** Arrange sliced Bond Roll on rectangular plate, 2 pieces side by side and 4 across. Pool the Bond sauce next to the arranged roll, and finish the plate with radish sprouts. Serve immediately.

*This roll can also be made without the salmon as a great vegetarian option.*

*GREMOLATA*

½ ounce garlic

½ ounce parsley

½ ounce lemon zest


*BOQUERONES NIGIRI*

½ ounce sushi rice

   (See page 79 for recipe.)

2 boquerones*

Bottagra for garnish**

*Boquerones are Spanish white anchovies. You can find these at specialty food stores.*

**Bottagra is cured fish roe. It can be found in specialty food stores or Asian markets.*

UCHI TIPS

**HOW TO ROLL**
Sushi rolls are meant to be delicate, not dense. So you need to gently squeeze when you're making them. They're meant to be eaten with your hands in Japan, and they are supposed to fall apart in your mouth. When you roll them too tight, they lose that light quality.

# BOQUERONES NIGIRI

MOST OF THE FISH WE USE AT UCHI IS JAPANESE, BUT WE LOVE BEING ABLE TO USE FISH FROM AROUND THE WORLD. THE BOQUERONES ARE SPANISH WHITE ANCHOVIES. WE BUY THEM CURED AND PICKLED. PAUL QUI STARTED MAKING PIECES OF SUSHI WITH THEM AND PEOPLE REALLY LOVE THEM, SO WE ADDED THEM TO THE PERMANENT MENU.

**FOR THE GREMOLATA:** Peel and grate the garlic. Finely chop the parsley. Combine with zest, mix well, and reserve for use.

**ASSEMBLY:** Make a dango, or dumpling shape, with the sushi rice. Place the boquerones on top of the rice. Top the piece with shaved bottagra and finish with gremolata zest.

BOQUERONES NIGIRI

# CRUNCHY TUNA ROLL

## THE REASON EVERY RESTAURANT HAS A SPICY TUNA ROLL IS BECAUSE IT'S THE MOST POPULAR SUSHI BAR ITEM. WE LIKE TO USE A GOOD CUT OF TUNA, FROM THE LOIN OF THE FISH, AND ADD CRUNCHY TEMPURA FLAKES TO GIVE IT A TWIST. ALL FOUR WORDS ASSOCIATED WITH THIS DISH MAKE IT A POPULAR ORDER: SPICY, CRUNCHY, TUNA, ROLL.

1 English cucumber

½ avocado

1 sushi-grade tuna loin

½ sheet nori paper

4 ounces sushi rice

White and black
   sesame seeds

**SPICY EMULSION**

1½ ounces negi

24 ounces kewpie
   mayonnaise

Splash of sesame oil

1¼ ounces momiji oroshi*

2½ ounces masago

Kosher salt to taste

*Momiji oroshi is a blend
of shredded daikon radish
and red chile peppers.
It can be found at most
Asian markets.*

**GARNISH**

1 ounce tempura flakes

Golden tobiko

**FOR THE ROLL:** Cut the cucumber in half crosswise. The halves should be at least 4 inches long. Cut the cucumber into quarters lengthwise. Place the cucumber skin side down, and run a sharp knife across the flesh to remove the seeds. Then cut the cucumbers again so that they are 4 inches by ½ inch by ½ inch. Reserve cucumber in the refrigerator. Quarter avocado lengthwise, peel, and remove the pit. With a sharp knife, slice avocado into ⅛-inch slices, wrap with plastic, and reserve in refrigerator until needed. Slice the tuna with a sharp knife into 4-inch by ½-inch by ½-inch slices.

Lay the shiny side of the nori down, the length facing you. Using damp fingers, apply the sushi rice to cover the nori. Leave about ½ inch of open strip at the top of the nori. Season the rice with sesame seeds. Flip the nori rice side down onto a plastic wrap–lined sushi mat. Place two portions of cucumber in the middle, end to end, and allow the cucumber to stick out on either end. Place the avocado slices with the cucumber from one edge of the nori to the other. Repeat the process with the tuna loin. Using the sushi mat as a guide, roll the rice-lined nori sheet up while pressing and gently squeezing the mat in toward you to shape the roll. Continue the process until the sushi roll is a tight uniform cylinder.

**FOR THE SPICY EMULSION:** Combine negi and kewpie mayonnaise in a food processor, and blend for 5 minutes to combine well. Transfer mix into a large stainless steel bowl. Add sesame oil, momiji oroshi, masago, and salt to the mixture, and whisk until well combined. Store in an airtight container for later use. Note: This recipe can be stored in the refrigerator and used for a number of different sushi dishes.

**ASSEMBLY:** Cover the sushi roll with tempura flakes, and cut into 8 pieces with a sharp knife. To make cutting easier and cleaner, dip the blade into cold water before slicing. Garnish the plate with golden tobiko and spicy emulsion.

UCHI TIPS

**DIFFERENT TYPES OF TUNA**
There are four or five different kinds of tuna. Most people are familiar with yellowfin tuna, which is also known as "ahi" tuna. Though it's popular in many restaurants as an appetizer that has been seared and dressed with some sort of soy-wasabi sauce, it's really not a very good fish for sushi. It's considered the lowest grade of tuna by the Japanese because it's not a deep-water tuna. It doesn't have a lot of fat, which means it doesn't have any flavor. If you just ate a raw piece of ahi tuna as sushi, it would be tasteless. For better tuna sushi, you have to get the tuna that swims in deeper water, like bigeye and bluefin.

# ENDO ROLL

THIS IS ATTRIBUTED TO A SUSHI CHEF I WORKED WITH NAMED YUYA ENDO. HIS NAME REMINDED ME OF AN "ENDO," WHICH IS A WHEELIE ON THE FRONT TIRE OF YOUR BICYCLE. SO THIS ROLL IS A SUSHI ROLL TURNED ON ITS HEAD, LIKE AN ENDO. INSTEAD OF RICE, WE USE RICE PAPER, AS WELL AS CREATIVE COMPONENTS LIKE FROZEN GRAPES AND UCHI FISH SAUCE.

*TEMPURA SHRIMP*

Vegetable oil, enough to
cover at least 2 inches in
a deep frying pan

1 shrimp per Endo roll

Tempura batter,
store bought

*PICKLED SHALLOTS*

12 ounces water

8 ounces sugar

4 ounces white wine
vinegar

1 cinnamon stick

2 star anise

½ ounce coriander seed

½ ounce black peppercorn

⅓ ounce kosher salt

6 shallots, thin sliced in
rounds on a mandolin

*PICKLED SHRIMP*

1 shrimp per Endo roll

Ice water bath

Pickling liquid from pickled
shallots

*THAI CHILE OIL*

5 ounces sambal

12 ounces vegetable oil

Rice paper

½ ounce lettuce

Cilantro

Basil

1 ounce frozen grapes, sliced

2 ounces fish sauce
(See page 80 for recipe.)

*FOR THE TEMPURA SHRIMP:* Bring oil to high heat for frying. (Avoid letting it get to smoking point.) Shell and devein shrimp. Stretch the shrimp lengthwise to double its length. Dip shrimp in tempura batter and fry in oil until golden. Remove from oil and reserve on a paper towel to cool down.

*FOR THE PICKLED SHALLOTS:* Add all ingredients except shallots into small sauce pot. Heat to boiling point. While pickling liquid is heating, thinly slice shallots, lengthwise. When liquid has come to a boil, strain through a fine mesh sieve over shallots. Leave at room temp to cool pickling shallots. Remove shallots for plating, and save the pickling liquid for the pickled shrimp.

*FOR THE PICKLED SHRIMP:* Bring a medium pot of water to a boil. Skewer the shrimp from head to tail under the shell along the belly, without piercing the meat. Boil the shrimp until they begin to float, and immediately pull and shock them in ice water. Peel and cut the head and tail off at a 45-degree angle. Along the belly, slice until you reach the intestine but not farther or you will break through to the other side, cutting the shrimp in half. You simply want to butterfly the shrimp and take out the intestine. Soak the shrimp in the shallot pickling liquid for 20 minutes.

*FOR THE THAI CHILE OIL:* Purée sambal and oil in blender for 8 minutes, refrigerate for at least 8 hours, then skim off solid, and reserve oil.

*ASSEMBLY:* Place a sheet of rice paper onto your cutting board, and using a spray bottle of water, lightly mist the paper. Lay leaves of mixed green lettuce end to end so that they lie slightly beyond of the ends of the rice paper. Place the tempura and pickled shrimp in the same pattern, and follow with cilantro and basil. Roll the rice paper and contents up tightly, and slice the roll into 6 pieces. Arrange the pieces on a rectangular plate. Place the pickled shallots and frozen grapes on top off the roll. In small bowls, place fish sauce and Thai chile oil, and serve beside roll.

UCHI TIPS

**USE A SHARP KNIFE**
When you make sashimi, you're slicing flesh, so the quality of the fish is extremely important, but so is the sharpness of the blade. If you use a dull blade, you're actually crushing something, not slicing it, which destroys the integrity of the fish. I had a sensei who said, "If your blade is sharp and you know how to use it, then you're taking something that is dead and bringing it back to life." You're giving life to the product and paying respect to it.

# FOIE GRAS NIGIRI

I HAD NEVER TRIED FOIE GRAS UNTIL I OPENED UCHI. I REALLY LIKED IT, BUT I DIDN'T WANT TO USE IT IN THE CONVENTIONAL WAY. I WANTED IT TO BE BITE-SIZE. SO WE CREATED A WAY FOR IT TO BE A PIECE OF NIGIRI, AND NOW IT'S ONE OF THE MOST POPULAR ORDERS AT THE RESTAURANT. WE FEATURED THIS FOR THE FIRST TIME AT THE TEXAS HILL COUNTRY WINE AND FOOD FESTIVAL A FEW YEARS AGO AND SERVED MORE THAN 1,000 ORDERS IN ONE NIGHT. PEOPLE WERE GOING CRAZY FOR IT.

**FOR THE CANDIED SHALLOT TARE:** Peel and thinly slice the shallots crosswise, about 1/16-inch slices. In a small sauce pot, combine sake, soy, mirin, and shallots and cook down to a syrup-like consistency. Remove from heat and let cool to room temperature. Reserve for later use.

**FOR THE CANDIED PORK BELLY:** Preheat oven to 325° F. Dice pork belly into ¼-inch pieces. In a small sauce pot, bring water and brown sugar to a boil. Let mixture boil for a few minutes to reduce the water content, making it a syrup-like consistency. Add diced pork belly, and cook on medium heat for about 10 minutes to ensure the belly is well coated and the syrup has cooked all the way through. Strain the pork belly out of the mixture, place on a silicon mat or a parchment-lined baking tray, and bake for 15 to 20 minutes or until pork belly is crispy, with a thin, sugary coating.

**FOR THE POMEGRANATE BOSHI:** Mix the yukari and sugar together and toss with the pomegranate seeds to coat well. Let sit for at least two hours. Remove seeds when ready to use.

**FOR THE FOIE GRAS:** In a hot sauté pan with a small amount of canola oil, sear the piece of foie gras until it fully caramelizes on one side. Remove and let rest on a paper towel.

**ASSEMBLY:** With damp fingers, make a dango, or dumpling, with 1 ounce sushi rice. Spoon a small amount of tare onto the rice. Place the foie gras on top of the dango lengthwise. Top with a small dollop of boshi and a piece of candied pork belly. Serve immediately.

**CANDIED SHALLOT TARE**

3 whole shallots

4 ounces sake

4 ounces soy sauce

4 ounces mirin

**CANDIED PORK BELLY**

8 ounces pork belly

6 ounces water

4 ounces brown sugar

**POMEGRANATE BOSHI**

1 ounce yukari flake

1 ounce sugar

1 ounce pomegranate seeds

Canola oil, enough to lightly coat sauté pan

1½ ounces foie gras

**SUSHI RICE**

(See page 79 for recipe.)

½ avocado

1 ounce hamachi

1 ounce unagi

½ nori sheet

4 ounces sushi rice

Golden tobiko

*BALSAMIC REDUCTION*

8 ounces high-quality
    balsamic vinegar

½ ounce sugar

*GARNISH*

Golden tobiko

# MUSTANG ROLL

THIS IS BASED ON A ROLL I USED TO MAKE AT MUSASHINO WITH YELLOWTAIL, EEL, AND EEL SAUCE. IT WAS DELICIOUS. AT UCHI, I WANTED TO MAKE A ROLL THAT WAS AN HOMAGE TO MUSASHINO, SO I TOOK THAT ROLL AND TWEAKED IT A LITTLE BIT BY ADDING SOME GOLDEN TOBIKO. I NAMED IT THE MUSTANG ROLL BECAUSE THE P-51 MUSTANG WAS MY FATHER'S FAVORITE WORLD WAR II PLANE.

*FOR THE MUSTANG ROLL:* Quarter avocado lengthwise, peel, and remove the pit. With a sharp knife, slice into ⅛-inch slices, wrap with plastic, and reserve in refrigerator until needed. Cut the hamachi against the grain into small strips. Grill the unagi to heat it through, and reserve for the roll. Lay the shiny side of the nori down, the length (the longer side) facing you. Using damp fingers, apply the sushi rice to cover the nori. Leave about ½ inch of open strip on the top of the nori. Flip the nori with rice onto a sushi mat lined with plastic wrap. Place rice side down so that nori is facing up. Place avocado in the middle, end to end, and the grilled unagi on top from end to end. Spread the portioned hamachi across the ingredients, and sprinkle the golden tobiko on top of the hamachi. Using the sushi mat as a guide, roll the rice-lined nori sheet up while gently squeezing the mat in toward you to shape the roll. Continue the process until the sushi roll is a tight uniform cylinder. Sprinkle the sushi roll with a little more tobiko and cut into 8 pieces with a sharp knife. To make cutting easier and cleaner, dip the blade into cold water before slicing.

*FOR THE BALSAMIC REDUCTION:* Reduce balsamic by about ½ and then add sugar. Continue to reduce the balsamic and sugar by another ½ and remove from heat. The consistency should be similar to maple syrup. Reserve for later use.

*ASSEMBLY:* Place 8 pieces of the sushi roll on the plate side by side lengthwise. Streak the plate with the balsamic reduction running parallel to the roll. Finish plate with a sprinkle of golden tobiko.

# PITCHFORK ROLL

EVERY JAPANESE RESTAURANT HAS SOME ROLL MADE WITH BEEF. WE WERE PLAYING AROUND WITH SOME WAGYU BEEF, AND I WANTED TO ADD A CRUNCHY TEXTURE TO THE OUTSIDE. I TRIED FRIED ONIONS, SCALLIONS, AND FINALLY LEEKS. WE MADE A SORT OF HAY OUT OF THE FRIED LEEKS, SO WE CALLED IT THE PITCHFORK ROLL AS A PLAY ON USING A PITCHFORK TO STACK HAY.

**FOR THE PITCHFORK ROLL:** Quarter avocado lengthwise, peel, and remove the pit. With a sharp knife, slice into ⅛-inch slices, wrap with plastic, and reserve in refrigerator until needed. Grill the flank steak on a hot grill. You want to get a hard sear on the outside while keeping the steak near rare/medium rare. Lay the shiny side of the nori down and the length (the longer side) facing you. Using damp fingers, apply the sushi rice to cover the strip of nori. Leave about ½ inch of open strip on the top of the nori. Flip the nori sheet with rice onto a sushi mat lined with plastic wrap with the rice side down. Place sliced avocado in the middle, end to end, and the grilled meat on top of the avocado. Spread a generous pinch of yuzu kosho across the ingredients. Using the sushi mat as a guide, roll the rice-lined nori sheet up while pressing and gently squeezing the mat in toward you to shape the roll. Continue the process until the sushi roll is a tight uniform cylinder. Sprinkle the sushi roll with tonburi, and cut into 8 pieces with a sharp knife. To make cutting easier and cleaner, dip the blade into cold water before slicing.

**FOR THE CRISPY LEEKS:** Remove stalky greens from bottom white part of leek. With a sharp knife, remove the root bottom part of the leek. Take the cleaned white part of leek and split it in half lengthwise. Cut leek again crosswise so that you have 4 uniform stacks of leek. Slice the leeks in a chiffonade, going along the grain of the leek. (You must use a very sharp knife to achieve the best results.) Slice all 4 quarters of the leeks, and rinse well with cold water to wash off any dirt and sediment. Toss the cut leeks with kosher salt and let sit for 15 minutes to break down some of the stringiness of the leek. Rinse the leeks of all the salt and use a lint-free kitchen towel to wring out, getting the slices as dry as possible. With a table-top fryer or a large sauce pot to create a stove-top fryer, heat fryer oil to 315° F. Toss the dried leek slices in cornstarch to coat, and shake off excess cornstarch to create a thin uniform coating. Fry the leeks, being careful not to overcrowd the fryer, until they are a light, golden brown. Remove the leeks from the fryer oil and place on paper towels to drain. Lightly sprinkle with salt and reserve in an airtight container for use.

**FOR THE PITCHFORK SAUCE:** Mince Thai chile. (You may remove seeds to make less spicy.) Peel garlic cloves and mince. Add the garlic and chile to the miso base and combine well. Add tamari and continue to mix well. Let the miso mixture sit overnight to infuse the flavors. After the sauce has infused, strain it through a fine mesh sieve to remove any pieces. With a handheld blender, finish the sauce by adding ½ teaspoon egg yolk and mixing well to smooth out purée.

**ASSEMBLY:** Arrange the sliced roll on the plate into 2 rows of 4 pieces, side by side. Add a couple of pools of pitchfork sauce to the plate. Finish the roll by topping it with a generous amount of the crispy leeks.

½ avocado

2 ounces wagyu flank steak

½ nori sheet

4 ounces sushi rice
(See page 79 for recipe.)

1 pinch yuzu kosho
(See page 76 for recipe.)

¼ ounce tonburi
(broom corn)

**CRISPY LEEKS**

1 leek

½ ounce kosher salt

2 ounces cornstarch

**PITCHFORK SAUCE**

1 Thai chile

2 cloves of garlic

5 ounces prepared
miso base
(See page 69 for recipe.)

¾ ounce tamari

½ teaspoon egg yolk

# SHAG ROLL

THIS IS ONE OF THE SIGNATURE UCHI ROLLS. I HAD A CUSTOMER WHO WANTED TO TRY SOMETHING DIFFERENT. HE WAS A REGULAR WHO OWNED A HAIR SALON CALLED SHAG. I DECIDED TO TAKE THE BOND ROLL AND FRY IT IN TEMPURA. I PAIRED IT WITH SOME SQUID INK AND SOME SUMISO SAUCE, WHICH IS MISO WITH VINEGAR. THAT WAS IT. HE LOVED IT AND TOLD EVERYONE ABOUT IT. IT WAS A PERMANENT MENU ITEM FROM THAT POINT ON.

## SUMISO

10 ounces miso base
   (See page 69 for recipe.)

½ ounce rice vinegar

¼ ounce squid ink

## ROLL

½ avocado

1 ounce salmon fillet

1 sun-dried tomato

½ sheet soy paper

3½ ounces sushi rice
   (See page 79 for recipe.)

Tempura batter (A store-bought version is sufficient. Follow directions for preparation.)

## SPICY EMULSION

1½ ounces negi

24 ounces kewpie mayonnaise

Splash of sesame oil

1¼ ounces momiji oroshi*

2½ ounces masago

Kosher salt to taste

*Momiji oroshi is a blend of shredded daikon radish and red chile peppers. It can be found at most Asian markets.

## GARNISH

Masago, or capelin roe

Black and white sesame seeds

**FOR THE SUMISO:** Combine miso base with vinegar and squid ink, and mix well with hand-held immersion blender. Store the sumiso in airtight container for later use.

**FOR THE SHAG ROLL:** Quarter avocado lengthwise, peel, and remove the pit. With a sharp knife, slice into ⅛-inch slices, wrap with plastic, and reserve in refrigerator until needed. Slice the salmon against the grain into small, thin slices. Julienne the sun-dried tomato. Lay the shiny side of the soy paper down, with the length (the longer side) facing you. Using damp fingers, apply the sushi rice to cover the strip of soy paper. Leave about ½ inch of open strip on the top of the soy paper. Place the rice-lined soy sheet onto a plastic wrap-lined sushi mat with the rice side up. Place sliced avocado in the middle, end to end, and the sliced salmon on top. Lay the sun-dried tomato on top of the avocado, being sure to get a consistent line on the ingredients. Using the sushi mat as a guide, roll the rice-lined soy paper sheet up while gently squeezing the mat in toward you to shape the roll. Continue the process until the sushi roll is a tight uniform cylinder. Dip the whole roll into tempura batter and place in a tabletop fryer at 350° F. Fry until the tempura batter has cooked all the way through, about 5 minutes. While the roll is frying, use your fingers to drizzle more tempura batter to coat the roll. Remove the roll from the fryer.

**FOR THE SPICY EMULSION:** Combine negi and kewpie mayonnaise in a food processor, and blend for 5 minutes to combine well. Transfer mix into a large stainless steel bowl. Add sesame oil, momiji oroshi, masago, and salt to the mixture, and whisk until well combined. Store in an airtight container for later use. Note: This recipe can be stored in the refrigerator and used for a number of different sushi dishes.

**ASSEMBLY:** Cut Shag Roll into 8 pieces. To make cutting easier and cleaner, dip the blade into cold water before slicing. Place together side by side, lengthwise on a rectangular plate. Place a dollop of spicy emulsion onto each piece of the roll. Streak the plate with the sumiso, and garnish with masago and black and white sesame seeds. Serve immediately.

UCHI TIPS

### TEMPURA

I don't really like a lot of fried foods. But the cool thing about tempura is that it's so light. The Japanese have a real serious love for tempura. There are restaurants completely devoted to it. Really good tempura is light, clean, and not greasy. And you can tempura anything—believe me, we've tried. We also use the leftover flakes from when we tempura something like our Shag Rolls to coat the Crunchy Tuna Roll, for example. It's a simple element for adding a light, flavorful crunch to a dish.

# ZERO SEN ROLL

**THIS IS BASED ON A CLASSIC COMBINATION OF SCALLION AND YELLOWTAIL, WITH A SAUCE THAT HAS SOME SPICE, ALONG WITH AVOCADO AND CRISPY SHALLOTS. THE SAUCE MAKES IT A LITTLE EDGY COMPARED TO AN AVERAGE JAPANESE ROLL. SO I NAMED IT A ZERO SEN, WHICH IS A JAPANESE KAMIKAZE PLANE FROM WORLD WAR II.**

1 ounce avocado

1 ounce hamachi

½ nori sheet

4 ounces sushi rice
   (see page 79 for recipe.)

1 pinch yuzu kosho

A few sprigs cilantro

Sprinkle golden tobiko

*MISO PURÉE*

1 Thai chile

2 cloves of garlic

5 ounces prepared
   miso base
   (see page 69 for recipe)

¾ ounce tamari

½ teaspoon of egg yolk

*CRISPY SHALLOTS*

1 quart soybean oil
   for frying

1 whole shallot

1 ounce all-purpose flour

Kosher salt to taste

*GARNISH*

Thai chile oil

Radish sprouts

Golden tobiko

**FOR THE ZERO SEN ROLL:** Quarter avocado lengthwise, peel, and remove the pit. With a sharp knife, slice into ⅛-inch slices, wrap with plastic, and reserve in refrigerator until needed. Slice the hamachi against the grain, into bite-size slices. Lay the shiny side of the nori down, the length (the longer side) facing you. Using damp fingers, apply the sushi rice to cover the strip of nori. Leave about ½ inch of open strip on the top of the nori. Place the rice-lined nori sheet onto a sushi mat lined with plastic wrap. Leave the rice side up. Place sliced avocado in the middle, end to end. Place the sliced hamachi on top of the avocado. Spread a pinch of yuzu kosho atop the ingredients, being sure to get a consistent line on the ingredients. Place cilantro leaves on top of the ingredients, and sprinkle golden tobiko as well. Using the sushi mat as a guide, roll the nori sheet up while pressing and gently squeezing the mat in toward you to shape the roll. Continue the process until the sushi roll is a tight uniform cylinder. With a sharp knife, slice the roll into 8 pieces. To make cutting easier and cleaner, dip the blade into cold water before slicing.

**FOR THE MISO PURÉE:** Mince Thai chile. (You may remove seeds to make less spicy.) Peel garlic cloves, and mince. Combine garlic and chiles with the miso base. Add tamari and continue to mix well. Let mixture sit overnight to infuse the flavors of the garlic and Thai chile. After the sauce has infused, strain it through a fine mesh sieve to remove pieces. With a handheld blender, finish the sauce by adding egg yolk, and mix well to smooth out purée.

**FOR THE CRISPY SHALLOTS:** In a deep saucepan, heat oil to 325° F. While oil is heating, slice across the shallot to make rings, about ¹⁄₁₆ inch in width. In a mixing bowl, toss the sliced shallots with the flour and pat to remove excess flour. Fry shallots in the oil and remove when golden brown, 45 seconds to 1 minute. Place fried shallots on paper towels to drain excess oil, and salt while warm. Store in an airtight container for later use.

**ASSEMBLY:** Arrange the sliced roll on the plate into 2 rows of 4 pieces, side by side. Finish the plate with pools of miso purée and a few drizzles of Thai chile oil. Garnish the plate with radish sprouts and a little more golden tobiko.

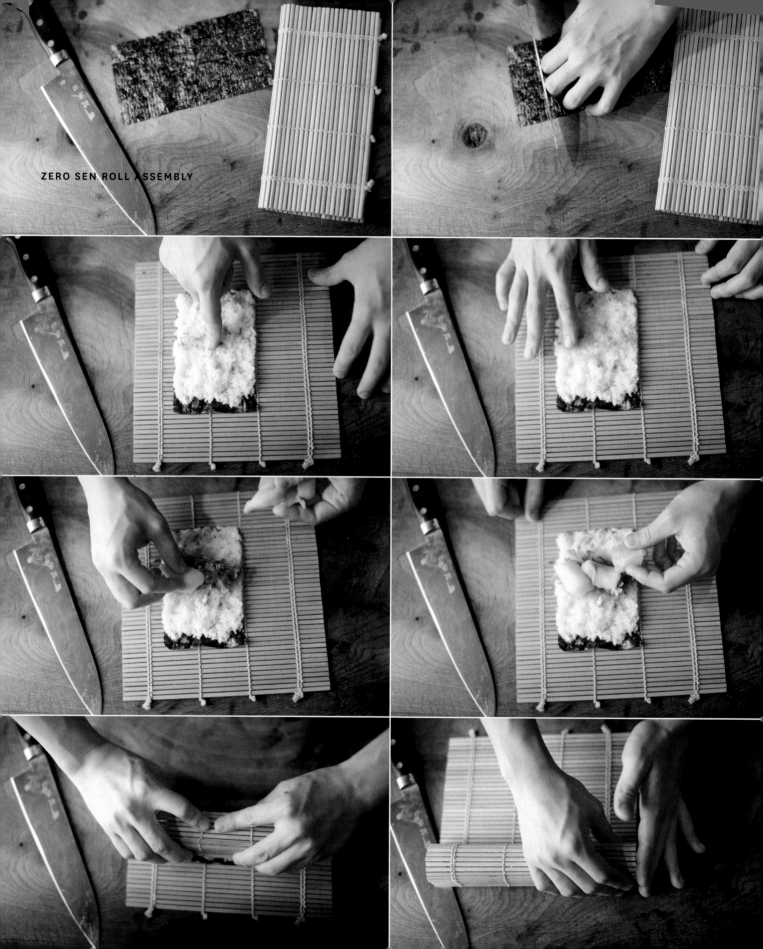

ZERO SEN ROLL ASSEMBLY

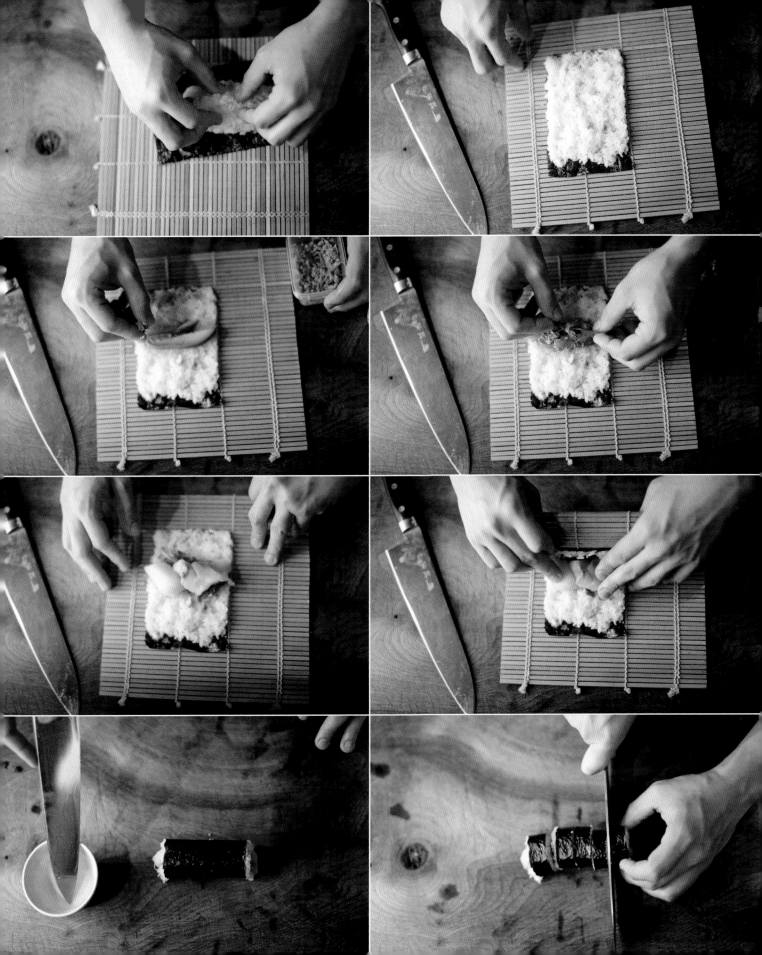

# TASTINGS

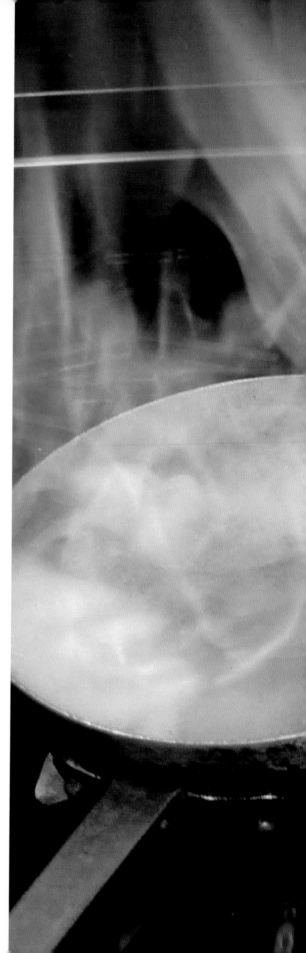

# A SMALL TASTE

Tastings is one of the permanent sections of the menu. The idea was to have hot and cold selections in tasting-size portions and for everything to be shared. People are just A.D.D. these days, with so many different things demanding their attention, and food has become like that for them as well. Our Tastings menu plays to that mentality and allows people to try a little bit of a lot of things. We wanted to offer hot and cold options to alternate as they are served. Something hot tastes so good when it's followed by something cold, sort of like warm apple pie and cold ice cream. Serving smaller portions also allows us to manage the quality of what we're putting out. When things are in smaller portions, I can really control the consistency and the integrity of the dish with the textures, temperature, and flavor.

**RECIPE NOTE**

These recipes are designed for a single serving. As with our Daily Specials, our Tastings are designed to be shared. Recipes can be adjusted if you are serving a large number of people.

# BACON STEAKIE

**THIS STARTED AT UCHI AS A SPECIAL. WE WANTED TO HAVE PORK BELLY ON THE MENU, BUT AT THE TIME, PORK BELLY WASN'T QUITE APPETIZING TO PEOPLE. IT HADN'T TAKEN OFF IN AUSTIN LIKE IT HAD IN NEW YORK OR LOS ANGELES. SO WE TRIED SOME DIFFERENT TECHNIQUES TO MAKE IT CRISPY AND DECIDED TO FRY AND CANDY IT AND SLICE IT THIN. INSTEAD OF CALLING IT PORK BELLY, WE CALLED IT BACON, AND WE ADDED THE WORD "STEAK" BECAUSE EVERYONE LOVES STEAK IN TEXAS. "STEAKIE" IS ALSO A PLAY ON A JAPANESE WORD THAT MEANS SOMETHING IS BADASS, WHICH THIS DISH REALLY IS. WE SELL MORE THAN 40 ORDERS A NIGHT.**

*PORK BELLY*

2 teaspoons sugar

1 teaspoon salt

1 pinch ground coriander

1 pinch ground juniper

5 ounces pork belly

Vegetable oil

Corn starch (enough to
   dust and coat the pork
   belly for frying)

*FISH CARAMEL*

(See page 59 for recipe.)

*THAI BASIL PURÉE*

3 garlic cloves

1 whole shallot

6 ounces vegetable oil

Kosher salt to taste

1 ounce Thai basil leaves

Ice water bath

Pinch citric acid

*SHAVED WATERMELON
RADISH*

1 watermelon radish

Ice water bath

*GARNISH*

1 serrano pepper, sliced
   into 1/16-inch rounds

1 kumquat, sliced into
   1/16-inch rounds

Lime juice

Olive oil

Salt

Thai basil

**FOR THE PORK BELLY:** Set up the immersion circulator at 164° F. Mix the sugar, salt, and spices together. Season the pork belly well with the cure mix, and seal in a vacuum bag. Place the bag in the circulator, making sure it is completely submerged. Cook overnight for 12 hours. Remove and let cool. (Note: An immersion circulator is a commercial-grade appliance. You can substitute this method by tightly sealing the pork belly in a sealable plastic bag and submerging it in a pot of 164° F water. You will need to continue to add water through the 12-hour cooking process, as it will evaporate from the pot.)

Preheat oven to broil. Heat a frying pan with vegetable oil over high heat. Dust the pork belly in corn starch and fry until golden, 3 to 4 minutes. Remove and glaze with fish caramel, and place in oven until heated through, 5 to 7 minutes. Slice and plate.

**FOR THE THAI BASIL PURÉE:** Peel and rough chop garlic and shallot to a uniform size. In a small sauté pan, gently sweat the garlic and shallots in about 1 ounce of vegetable oil over low heat. Add a pinch of kosher salt to help bring out the flavors from the garlic and shallot. While garlic is heating, bring a small sauce pot of salted water to a boil. Prepare an ice bath for shocking the basil after it is blanched.

Blanch basil leaves in boiling water for about 30 seconds, and then immediately shock them in the ice bath. Remove and place on paper towels to soak up excess water. Place sweated shallot and garlic, with cooking oil, into a stainless bowl on ice bath to cool down. In a blender, purée oil mixture, remaining oil, blanched basil, salt, and citric acid. Keep oil as cool as possible while blending to prevent purée from turning color. Once all ingredients are consistently puréed, remove from blender and cool down on ice bath. Reserve the basil purée at room temperature for later use.

**FOR THE WATERMELON RADISH:** With a peeler, shave the radish into paper-thin slices. Place shaved radish into a container with ice water to shock it and give it a more toothsome texture. Use immediately.

**ASSEMBLY:** On a rectangular plate, place a 2-inch strip of fish caramel down first, followed by the sliced pork belly. Using a squirt bottle, place three rounds of basil purée around the pork belly. In a stainless bowl, combine radish, serranos, and kumquats, and dress with a drizzle of lime juice and olive oil and a dash of salt to taste. Top the pork belly with salad and garnish with Thai basil.

2½ ounces Japanese
    sea bass
1 clove garlic, finely
    chopped

*ORANGE OIL*
Zest of 2 large oranges
2 ounces vegetable oil

*SAN BAI ZU*
(See page 80 for recipe.)

*YUZU PON SAUCE*
(See page 80 for recipe.)

*GARNISH*
Black pepper
Maldon salt
Micro arugula
Golden tobiko

# CRUDO

THIS IS A SIMPLE DISH USING SUZUKI, A SMALL JAPANESE STRIPED SEA BASS THAT IS REALLY CLEAN AND CRISP. IT'S A GREAT EXAMPLE OF THE KIND OF SUSHI I LIKE TO MAKE. WHEN I STARTED PLAYING WITH DIFFERENT COMPONENTS TO ADD TO THIS FISH, I FOUND THAT SIMPLY ADDING SOME BRUNOISED GARLIC TO A TANGERINE-INFUSED OIL AND MALDON SALT MADE THE PERFECT COMBINATION. I LOVE USING ONLY A FEW SIMPLE INGREDIENTS TO MAKE A PERFECT PIECE OF FISH EVEN BETTER, AND THE CRUDO IS AN EXAMPLE OF HOW WE ACHIEVED THAT.

**FOR THE JAPANESE SEA BASS:** Use ½ a side of cleaned and scaled sea bass. Score the skin side of the fish in a crosshatch pattern. Slice the fish across the grain into about 6 slices, and keep the pieces of the fish together so that the shape of the fillet is intact. Reserve in a clean chilled stainless steel bowl in refrigerator. Brunoise the clove of garlic and reserve.

**FOR THE ORANGE OIL:** Place the zest into the vegetable oil and reserve in a warm place overnight to infuse maximum flavor. Strain the zest from the mixture.

**ASSEMBLY:** Place the sliced fish in the center of a chilled shallow bowl. Dress the plate with the san bai zu and yuzu pon sauce, and place drops of orange oil around the fish. On top of the fish, line the garlic, black pepper, and maldon salt down the middle of the fish. Garnish with a few leaves of micro arugula and a sprinkle of golden tobiko, and serve.

# HIRAME USUZUKURI

**HIRAME IS FLOUNDER. IT'S ONE OF THE FIRST PIECES OF RAW FISH I EVER TRIED. I HAD IT WITH PONZU AT NIPPON JAPANESE RESTAURANT IN HOUSTON. THE TEXTURE AND ACIDITY WERE JUST PERFECT. IT'S STILL ONE OF THE FAVORITE MEMORIES I'VE HAD WITH SUSHI, AND I WANTED TO HAVE THE DISH ON THE UCHI MENU. WE "UCHI-FIED" IT WITH CRISPY CHIPS MADE FROM THE FLOUNDER AND FRIED CANDIED QUINOA, AND WE SLICED THE FLOUNDER SUPER THIN, WHICH IS THE BEST WAY TO EAT IT.**

*FRIED FLOUNDER*
*BODY CHIPS*

1 cup soybean oil

1 whole flounder body

Salt

*CRISPY QUINOA*

(See page 59 for recipe.)

*SAN BAI ZU*

(See page 80 for recipe.)

*GARNISH*

Olive oil

½ teaspoon yuzu juice

1 tablespoon daikon,
    finely shredded

Tobiko

Smoked sea salt to taste

Pinch of yuzu zest

*FOR THE FRIED FLOUNDER BODY CHIPS:* Pour oil into pan and heat to 325° F. Remove head and fillets from the body of the flounder. Fry the whole body, with the spine and fins still intact, until golden brown. Remove from oil and let sit on paper towels to absorb excess oil. Salt the fried fish body. Break off pieces of the fins into small chips and reserve. Reserve fish body for serving.

*ASSEMBLY:* On chilled plate, lay thinly sliced flounder pieces side by side, slightly overlapping each other. Sprinkle a tablespoon of crispy quinoa over fish and on plate. Spoon san bai zu around the circumference of the chilled plate.

Next, drizzle olive oil around circumference of plate. Add a sprinkle of yuzu juice, and place a large pinch of finely shredded daikon on top of fish and quinoa. Sprinkle the plate and the daikon mound with tobiko. Finish with a pinch of smoked sea salt and yuzu zest, and garnish with fried flounder body chips.

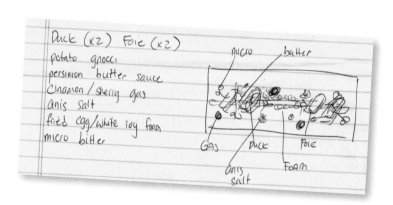

4 ounces fresh baby squid

6 ounces kimchee base
(See page 67 for recipe.)

# IKA YAKI

SQUID SALADS ARE FAIRLY POPULAR AT JAPANESE RESTAURANTS, BUT A LOT OF THEM ARE JUST PREPACKAGED VERSIONS THAT ARE DEFROSTED AND SERVED. MANY PEOPLE LIKE THEM BECAUSE THEY HAVE GREAT TEXTURE AND A LOT OF FLAVOR. WE WANTED TO HAVE OUR OWN VERSION OF SQUID SALAD THAT RAISED THE BAR. SO WE BROUGHT IN FRESH SQUID, WHICH WE MARINATE AND GRILL, AND ADDED TOMATOES AND CURRY GASTRIQUE. IT'S A REAL FRESH DISH THAT A LOT OF PEOPLE LOVE.

*CURRY APPLE GASTRIQUE*

8 ounces apple juice

8 ounces white vinegar

¼ ounce red curry paste

¼ ounce sugar

*COMPRESSED GREEN TOMATO*

1 green tomato

1 ounce Uchi fish sauce
(See page 80 for recipe.)

*SALAD AND GARNISH*

1 Granny Smith apple

1 head of baby romaine lettuce

Kosher salt to taste

½ ounce apple curry gastrique

**FOR THE SQUID:** Clean the squid, place in kimchee base, and marinate for at least 8 hours or overnight. Place squid over high heat on a grill and let cook for about 1 minute, to achieve a sear. Lower the heat to medium or move the squid to a cooler part of the grill to finish the cooking process. Flip the squid after another 2 minutes and continue to cook for 3 minutes. Once the squid is fully cooked, remove from the grill and let it rest briefly while composing the rest of the dish.

**FOR THE CURRY APPLE GASTRIQUE:** Combine all ingredients in a medium saucepan and mix well to combine. Reduce over medium-low heat until the sauce reaches a syrup-like consistency.

**FOR THE COMPRESSED GREEN TOMATO:** Slice tomato into rounds about ⅜ inch thick. Place tomatoes and fish sauce in a vacuum seal bag and follow manufacturer's directions.

**ASSEMBLY:** With a mandolin, slice ¼ of an apple at about ¹⁄₁₆ inch thick and reserve. Break the romaine lettuce leaves away from the stalk and reserve. Slice compressed green tomatoes into narrow strips and reserve. Cut grilled and rested squid into ½-inch-thick rings and reserve. In a medium stainless bowl, toss together the apples, tomatoes, squid, romaine leaves, and a pinch of kosher salt. Place the tossed ingredients onto a rectangular plate in a linear fashion. Drizzle the curry apple gastrique on top, and serve immediately.

IKA YAKI

# KONA KANPACHI

THE KEY TO THIS DISH IS THE NABE, WHICH IS A JAPANESE HOT POT. WE HEAT IT ON THE STOVE TOP TO GET IT REALLY HOT AND ASSEMBLE THIS WITH A VARIETY OF TEXTURES, INCLUDING SUSHI RICE—WHICH GETS CRISPY IN THE BOWL—SCALLION, EGG YOLK, BONITO FLAKES, AND THE KANPACHI, WHICH IS A YOUNG YELLOW-TAIL. THE SMELL OF IT IS AMAZING, AND THE BONITO FLAKES SORT OF WAVE AROUND FROM THE HEAT OF THE BOWL. IT'S DELICIOUS.

**FOR THE KANPACHI SAUCE:** Heat sake in medium saucepan and burn off alcohol, about 2 minutes. Remove from heat. Combine remaining ingredients and simmer for 10 minutes. Remove from heat and let steep for 15 minutes.

**FOR THE SESAME RELISH:** Brunoise the garlic and shallot, and thinly slice the Thai chile in rounds. Mix the vegetables with the oils. Reserve for service.

**ASSEMBLY:** Heat a nabe, or Japanese hot pot, on the stove with a little bit of oil. Toss diced kanpachi with the sesame relish and season with salt and pepper. Just before the oil reaches its smoking point, add the rice. Next add the kanpachi. Top with egg yolk and sprinkle of furikake, bonito flakes, and diced negi. Serve with a side of kanpachi sauce.

1 ounce vegetable oil

2 ounces kanpachi, diced

Salt and pepper

1 cup cooked sushi rice

**KANPACHI SAUCE**

5 ounces sake

7 ½ ounces mirin

5 ounces soy

½ ounce dashi

1 ounce garlic

**SESAME RELISH**

2 ounces garlic

3 ounces shallot

½ ounce Thai chile

2 ounces sesame oil

6 ounces vegetable oil

**GARNISH**

1 egg yolk

Furikake*

Bonito flakes

¼ stalk negi, diced

*Furikaki is Japanese seasoning mix commonly found at Asian markets.*

UCHI TIPS

**DASHI**

Dashi is a mysterious ingredient. It is one of the main elements of Japanese cuisine, made from a concentrated broth of kombu (kelp) and katsuobushi (bonito flakes). Most Japanese households use hon dashi, which comes in a bottle and looks like little pieces of bullion. Just the hon dashi mixed with warm water makes the most delicious broth. Most Japanese restaurants put that in their miso soup. Add a little bit of it to just about anything—fish, soup, even watermelon—and it brings out fantastic flavors.

# MACHI CURE

WE CAME UP WITH THIS WHEN WE WERE MESSING AROUND WITH DIFFERENT INGREDIENTS FOR CHIPS. WE HAD YUCCA ROOT, AND WE LIKED HOW WELL A THIN YUCCA CHIP WORKED WITH SASHIMI. WE ADDED SOME YELLOWTAIL THAT WE HAD CURED AND SMOKED TO GIVE IT A SALTY SWEETNESS. THEN WE ADDED CRUNCHY MARCONA ALMONDS AND CANDIED GARLIC AND CONTRASTED THAT WITH GOLDEN RAISINS. A LOT OF PEOPLE CALL THESE JAPANESE NACHOS, WHICH IS PRETTY FITTING.

**SMOKED HAMACHI**
24 ounces sugar
8 ounces kosher salt
3 to 5 cinnamon sticks
½ ounce cloves
½ ounce juniper berries
1 fillet hamachi
    (yellowtail)
2 ounces applewood chips,
    soaked 15 to 20 minutes

**YUCCA CHIP**
Soybean oil, enough to
    coat 2 inches of a pan
1 large yucca root
    (at least 24 ounces)
Salt

**GARNISH**
½ clove garlic
½ Asian pear
½ ounce golden raisins
½ ounce Marcona almonds
1 splash white soy
2 drops orange-infused oil
1 pinch of micro chervil

**FOR THE SMOKED HAMACHI:** Place sugar and salt in large mixing bowl. Combine cinnamon, cloves, and juniper in a kitchen towel and crush with the back of a knife. Then place in a spice grinder until finely ground. Mix well with sugar and salt mixture. To prepare the fish for smoking, cut it down the middle between the pin bones. Remove the rib cage from the belly side and place it in a sheet pan. Trim all dark meat from the other half of the fish and add it to the sheet pan. Pour a generous amount of curing mixture over the fish and let cure, covered, in refrigeration for at least 2 to 3 hours. Remove excess cure from the fish, but be sure to leave a little on the surface. That will help the smoke hang on to the fish and add nice flavor. To smoke, fill a hotel pan or 9 x 13 baking pan with ice. Place the fish on top of the ice and place the half pan inside a deeper hotel pan. Add applewood chips to one side of the larger pan and cover with a hotel pan of equal size to create a closed box for smoking. Place the "smoking box" on the stove, making sure that only the side with the wood is exposed to the heat. Smoke on high for 7 minutes, then remove from heat and let smoke for additional 3 minutes. Remove from the smoker and let chill before serving.

**FOR THE YUCCA CHIP:** In a table-top fryer, or in a large sauce pot, heat oil to 350° F. With a mandolin, slice the yucca lengthwise to 1/16 inch thick. Fry the chips, a few at a time, in order to allow maximum oil coverage. You do not want them overlapping. Fry until they have caramelized to a slight golden brown, but do not let the color get too dark. Flip the chips halfway through the process to achieve an evenly fried chip. Remove from oil and place on paper towels to drain excess oil. Slightly salt chips while still warm. Reserve for later use.

**ASSEMBLY:** With a very sharp knife, slice smoked hamachi into ¼-inch slices. Place the sliced fish into a cold stainless bowl and reserve over ice. Dice the garlic into 1/16-inch pieces and reserve. Slice the Asian pear into ¼-inch slices and reserve with hamachi. In the same bowl, toss the fish, pear, raisins, and almonds with the white soy and orange oil. Add the diced garlic and toss well to coat. To serve, on a chilled plate, place one chip down with a piece of the sliced fish and pear on top. Add a bit of the almonds and raisins. Alternately layer chips with the pear, fish, raisins, and almonds. Garnish plate with a bit of orange oil and micro chervil.

4 to 6 ounces water

¼ ounce green tea

½ ounce hon dashi*

8 ounces cooked rice

Kosher salt to taste

Pinch of radish sprouts

Pinch of bonito flakes

1 scallion, julienned

¼ sheet of nori, sliced into
  very thin strips

*Hon dashi is a type of
Japanese fish soup stock
that can be found at most
Asian food markets.

# OCHA ZUKE BROTH

THIS IS SOMETHING THAT'S DEAR TO ME; IT SYMBOLIZES EVERYTHING I LOVE ABOUT JAPANESE FOOD. IT'S SOMETHING PEOPLE EAT FOR BREAKFAST IN JAPAN. IT'S GREEN TEA, FRESH WHITE RICE, AND USUALLY SOME KIND OF GRILLED FISH. IT'S NOT SOMETHING YOU'D EVER THINK OF EATING IN AMERICA FOR BREAKFAST. THE FIRST TIME I HAD IT WAS IN JAPAN, WITH SNAPPER, AND THE COMBINATION OF FLAVORS JUST GOT BETTER AND BETTER AS I ATE IT. I FELT GOOD ALL DAY LONG AFTER EATING IT. THE INGREDIENTS ARE SO HEALTHY AND PURE. IT'S THE PERFECT WAY TO START THE DAY.

**ASSEMBLY:** Heat water on medium-low. Add tea and dashi and simmer for 10 minutes. Remove from heat and strain into a bowl with a scoop of rice. Season to taste with salt. Garnish with radish sprouts, bonito flakes, scallions and nori.

# PORK BELLY ONIGIRI

ONIGIRI IS BASICALLY A BIG RICE BALL. IT'S WHAT A LOT OF JAPANESE KIDS EAT FOR LUNCH AT SCHOOL. JAPANESE WOMEN WILL USE LEFT-OVER RICE AND FISH OR ANOTHER PROTEIN AND STUFF IT INSIDE OF A RICE BALL. I'VE MADE A THOUSAND VERSIONS OF THIS, BUT WITH THE PORK BELLY VERSION, WE MIX THE RICE WITH BONITO FLAKES AND SCALLIONS FOR FLAVOR. WE TAKE PORK BELLY, PRESS RICE AROUND IT TO FORM A BALL, AND THEN WE FRY IT. WE ALWAYS SERVE IT WITH A SWEET COMPONENT FOR ACCENT. IT'S SUCH A SURPRISE, CRISPY ON THE OUTSIDE AND SOFT ON THE INSIDE, AND PEOPLE REALLY LOVE IT.

**FOR THE CHILE SAUCE BASE:** Combine the salt, sugar, and chile flakes, and mix well. Combine fish sauce, water, and vinegar, and mix well. Pour the vinegar mixture into the sugar mixture, and mix well. Slice the negi whites into thin rounds, cutting across the stalk. Peel and slice the garlic thinly, across the grain. Add the garlic and negi to mixture, and mix well. Refrigerate for later use.

**FOR THE BANH MI PICKLES:** Heat the chile base until it is warmed through but below the boiling point. Slice the cucumber and carrots on a mandolin about ⅛ inch thick. Pour the warmed chile base over the sliced cucumbers and carrots, and let sit overnight. Refrigerate to reserve.

**FOR THE ONIGIRI RICE:** Preheat pan with oil to 325° F. Mix the sushi rice with negi, bonito flake, furikake, white soy, and sesame oil. Mix well to incorporate flavors, being careful not to overwork the rice. Ball the sushi rice with a ½-ounce portion of pork belly in the center of the ball. Fry until the rice becomes golden and crispy and the centers are heated through.

**ASSEMBLY:** Slice the onigiri balls in half and place on a small square plate. Place the pickles in between the halves and top with cilantro. Place a small ramekin of tamari on the plate for dipping.

1 ounce pork belly,
    cut in two

**CHILE SAUCE BASE**
Kosher salt to taste
2 ounces sugar
½ ounce Korean chile flake
2 ounces fish sauce
½ ounce water
2 ounces white vinegar
1 ounce negi whites
1 ounce garlic

**BANH MI PICKLES**
8 ounces chile sauce base
9 ounces cucumber
3.5 ounces carrots

**ONIGIRI RICE**
Vegetable oil, enough to
    cover 2 inches of
    frying pan
6¼ ounces sushi rice
½ ounces negi, chopped
1 pinch bonito flake
¼ ounce furikake*
¼ ounce white soy
Splash of sesame oil

*Furikaki is Japanese
seasoning mix commonly
found at Asian markets.

**GARNISH**
A few sprigs cilantro
2 ounces tamari

# SABA SHIO

**THIS MAY BE THE SIMPLEST DISH ON THE UCHI MENU. SABA IS MACKEREL. IT IS ONE OF THE FATTIEST FISH WE GET, BUT IF YOU COULD EAT ONE THING A DAY TO LIVE TO 100, IT SHOULD PROBABLY BE SABA. IT IS RICH WITH OMEGA 3 OILS. SABA SHIO IS SALTED AND GRILLED MACKEREL, AND WE SERVE IT WITH GRATED DAIKON OR PRESERVED LEMON TO CUT THE STRONG TASTE OF THE FISH.**

### SABA

4 ounces saba (mackerel)
    fillet

4 ounces salt

2 ounces dried kombu

8 ounces rice wine vinegar

Kosher salt and black
    pepper for grilling

### SABAZU

(See page 80 for recipe.)

### PRESERVED LEMON

2 whole lemons

4 ounces sugar

4 ounces kosher salt

### GARNISH

½ English cucumber,
    medium diced

Parsley

*FOR THE SABA:* Place the cleaned saba fillet, flesh side down, in salt. The salt should cover the whole flesh side of fish. Let the fillet cure for 30 minutes. Remove from salt and carefully rinse with cold water. (Saba flesh is fragile, so handle the fish gently.) Remove white sediment from dried kombu with a damp cloth. Place the saba fillet in a container and cover with rice wine vinegar and dried kombu. Let soak for 1 hour. Remove fish from vinegar and place onto clean, lint-free kitchen towel. With skin side up, gently peel off outer skin, starting at the belly side of the fish. Score the skin side in a small crisscross pattern, and reserve fish in the refrigerator.

*FOR THE PRESERVED LEMON:* Slice lemons crosswise about ⅛ inch thick. Mix sugar and salt in a medium bowl and toss lemon slices in mixture. Place lemons into a vacuum seal bag and pour remaining mixture into the bag. Vacuum seal according to manufacturer's instructions and let preserve for at least 1 hour. Remove lemons from bag and reserve for later use.

*ASSEMBLY:* To grill the saba, season scored side of fish with kosher salt and a pinch of fresh cracked black pepper. Place saba, seasoned side down, on the grill over medium-high heat. Sear for 1 minute and then move to medium heat, leaving the skin side down, and cook until the skin begins to get crispy. Once the skin is caramelized and has crispy edges, gently flip the saba and finish cooking on the flesh side; this should take just a few minutes. Remove saba from the grill and set aside. Place 2 ounces sabazu in a deep bowl and place grilled saba in pool. Lay preserved lemon wheels along the saba in a row. Place diced English cucumber along the side and on top of the saba, and finish with fresh picked parsley.

TORO NUTA

# TORO NUTA

THIS IS ANOTHER UCHI HOME RUN. I MADE IT FOR THE FIRST TIME FOR A CUSTOMER WHEN I WAS WORKING AT THE SUSHI BAR. HE WANTED ME TO MAKE HIM SOMETHING "DIFFERENT." I HAD SOME TORO, AND I WANTED TO PUT IT WITH SOMETHING THAT REMINDED ME OF GRANOLA. SO I COMBINED IT WITH SOME MARCONA ALMONDS AND DRIED CRANBERRIES AND ADDED A LITTLE GARLIC AND WHITE SOY SAUCE. IT WAS SOMETHING I JUST PUT TOGETHER ON THE FLY, BUT IT WAS INCREDIBLE. IT'S ANOTHER EXAMPLE OF HOW OUR CUSTOMERS REALLY PUSH US TO PUT OUT BETTER FOOD.

2 ounces bluefin tuna belly

1 clove garlic

1 stalk green onion

1 ounce white soy

½ ounce dried cranberries

½ ounce Marcona almonds

With a sharp knife, slice the tuna belly, against the grain, into 8 thin sashimi-style slices. Reserve in a chilled stainless steel bowl in the refrigerator. Brunoise the garlic clove and reserve. Slice the green onion, on a bias in very thin slices, no longer than ¼ inch. In the chilled stainless steel bowl, toss the tuna, green onion, and garlic with the ¾ ounce white soy to coat well. On a rectangular chilled sashimi plate, place the ingredients in a row, running parallel with the plate. Toss the cranberries and almonds with the remaining white soy and place across the plate. Serve immediately.

UCHI TIPS

**TORO TUNA**
Bluefin tuna swims the deepest and has the most fat, and therefore the most flavor. The best cut of meat from bluefin is the toro, or belly. It's like having a really good piece of wagyu beef. There are a few kinds of bluefin tuna, and they're endangered. The bluefin we get at the restaurant is southern bluefin, and it is sustainable. It comes from Perth on the west coast of Australia. While we do serve some toro, most of the tuna we serve at Uchi is bigeye. It has just enough fat and flavor and a great red flesh.

½ orange bell pepper,
   sliced into small strips
½ Thai chile pepper, sliced
   extra thin
4 small vine-ripened
   cherub tomatoes,
   halved
10 cilantro leaves
2 ounces whitefish (striped
   bass or red snapper)
2 ounces King salmon
½ clove fresh garlic,
   micro diced
Salt and fresh cracked
   black pepper to taste
1 tablespoon yuzu pon
   (See page 80 for recipe.)
1 tablespoon san bai zu
   (See page 80 for recipe.)
1 ounce arugula
   micro greens

# UCHIVICHE

HERE IS ANOTHER EXAMPLE OF MY OBSESSION WITH ACIDITY. FOR THE BEST FLAVOR COMBINATION, WE QUICKLY MARINATE THE FISH AND FRESH PEPPERS, CHILES, AND TOMATOES IN PONZU SAUCE. IT'S MY UCHI TWIST ON TRADITIONAL CEVICHE. TO ME, THE TYPICAL CEVICHE IS MARINATED FOR TOO LONG, TURNING OUT TOO STRONG, OVERCOOKED IN LIME JUICE, AND DRY. I PREFER FOR THE ACID TO ACCENTUATE THE FISH AND VEGETABLES RATHER THAN OVERCOOK IT. THIS DISH IS EN-TIRELY BASED ON TECHNIQUE AND QUALITY OF THE INGREDIENTS, AND WE'VE MADE A NUMBER OF VERSIONS OVER THE YEARS: MY FAVORITE WAS WITH SLICED RIPE TEXAS PEACHES AND YELLOW TEARDROP TOMATOES.

In a small chilled stainless steel bowl, mix together peppers, tomatoes, cilantro, fish, and garlic. Season with salt and pepper. Add half the yuzu pon and san bai zu. Gently toss ingredients together to combine. Place mixed ingredients on a chilled plate and dress with remaining yuzu pon and san bai zu. Garnish with micro arugula. (Can be made as a vegetarian dish, with fish omitted.)

# TUNA AND GOAT CHEESE SASHIMI

A FRIEND INTRODUCED ME TO PUMPKIN SEED OIL A LONG TIME AGO, AND I STARTED PUTTING IT ON EVERYTHING TO SEE WHAT WOULD GO WELL WITH IT. I REMEMBER DRIZZLING IT OVER SOME FUJI APPLES WITH A LITTLE SALT AT HOME, AND I LOVED IT. I TOOK IT TO UCHI AND ADDED SOME TUNA, AND IT WAS ALMOST PERFECT. IT JUST NEEDED A LITTLE FAT. SO WE ADDED GOAT CHEESE. THAT WAS THE LAST PIECE OF THE PUZZLE, AND AFTER THAT IT PRETTY MUCH BECAME THE SIGNATURE DISH ON UCHI'S MENU.

Slice Fuji apple into 8 thin wedges. Slice tuna into bite-size pieces and mix with apple in a chilled stainless bowl with cold san bai zu, salt, and pepper. Plate seasoned and dressed tuna and apples on chilled plate or in chilled bowl, and sprinkle with goat cheese. Add pumpkin seed oil to plate and garnish with micro red shiso. Finish with another pinch of kosher salt to taste.

¼ large Fuji apple, skin on
3 ounces big eye tuna
1 ounce san bai zu
   (See page 80 for recipe.)
Kosher salt and fresh
   cracked black pepper
   to taste
1½ ounces soft chevre
   goat cheese
2 teaspoons pumpkin
   seed oil
1 ounce red shiso
   micro greens

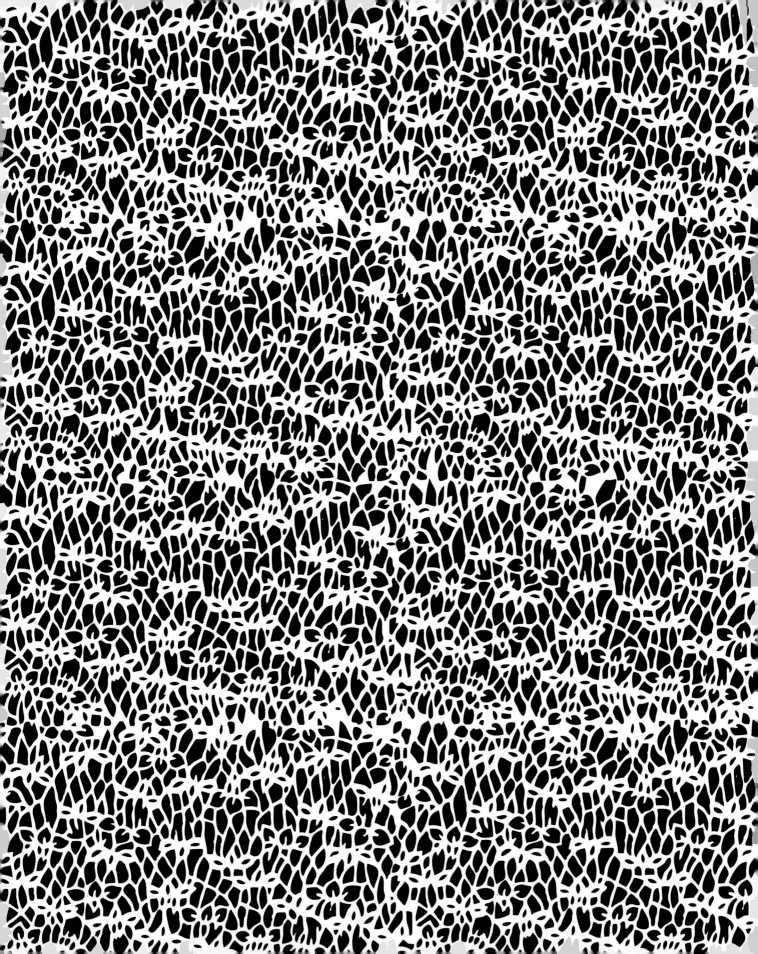

# DESSERTS

# A CLEAN FINISH

When we opened Uchi in 2003, desserts were an afterthought. I really wanted to make a great sushi bar. Honestly, I just didn't care about desserts. A lot of people say that desserts add value. Others say that desserts don't cost a lot of money and can keep people seated for another hour. That can ultimately subtract from your bottom line, and you may be better off flipping that table.

We had mochi ice cream and a few other things, but the idea of a pastry chef was beyond comprehension. After a few years in business, I started to change my mind. With all the momentum we had gained, I didn't think it looked good to ignore that part of the menu. At the same time, I didn't want our desserts to diverge from the Japanese aesthetic we had throughout the menu. I didn't want crème brulée or chocolate cake or apple pie. Those things have their place but not on my menu. I wanted our desserts to transition from the rest of the menu as a clean, fresh, palate-cleansing course. At first I tried to do things myself, but I didn't have anyone who could teach me. So finally, I decided that we really needed a pastry chef.

## PHILIP SPEER

I found Philip Speer while he was working at another Austin restaurant. He had a lot of experience and a great reputation, so I asked him to stage with us on a trial basis. It wasn't long before I realized how much he brought to the table. He had a rare ability to take some of the crazy ideas in my head and bring them to fruition. He'd try anything and pull it off.

Philip helped us work to establish some finite parameters for how our desserts would be designed as their own unique addition to the Uchi experience. They had to be fresh, crisp, clean. And they had to exhibit the same attention to taste, texture, and flavor that we give to the rest of the menu. Once we had those guidelines in place, he really hit a stride and our dessert menu took off.

I could come up with some crazy concept and ask him to make it, and without fail, he would figure out a way to do it. I'll never forget when we came up with brown butter sorbet. I had a dinner dish one night with brown butter, and I just had this thought that it could be great as a sorbet. So I called Phil and asked him to do it. At first he said it was impossible. Brown butter ice cream he could do, but sorbet? Sure enough, he spent days trying to make it work. And he did it. And it has turned out to be part of one of the most popular desserts we've ever had at the restaurant.

Usually, we work off of colors. I'll come up with a color for a dessert that I want to see on a plate, and Philip will go to work trying to make that happen. We'll use all sorts of ingredients you wouldn't expect, from peas to yellow corn. For a yellow dessert, he came up with our Polenta Custard, Corn Sorbet, Corn Milk, and Corn Flake Tuile. It's beautiful on the plate, and it tastes amazing.

Working our desserts is why we hired Philip, but he's taken a pivotal role in helping Paul Qui and me develop everything on our menu. The past few years have been a big part of his maturation process. Before, he was a pastry chef. Now he's a chef who helps oversee everything we put out. His success at Uchi has turned something that was once an afterthought as a menu item into a dedicated chapter in this book.

**RECIPE NOTE**

Each dessert recipe is assembled to reflect a single plating, as with our previous recipe sections. Many of these recipes yield enough to make a few servings if you wish to serve more than one.

## COFFEE MILK

16 ounces milk

4 ounces coffee beans

## MANGO YOLK

7 ounces mango purée

2 ounces water

2 ounces sugar

## COFFEE PANNA COTTA

2 sheets gelatin

Ice water

3 ounces coffee milk

½ teaspoon salt

3 ounces sugar

8 ounces heavy whipping
   cream

6 frozen mango yolks

## COFFEE SOIL

4½ ounces sugar

4½ ounces macadamia nuts

1 ounce cocoa powder

1 teaspoon salt

2⅓ ounces flour

1 ounce ground coffee beans

3½ ounces melted butter

## WHITE CHOCOLATE
## SORBET

12 ounces water

10 ounces sugar

½ teaspoon salt

2½ ounces white chocolate

## MANGO PAPER

4 ounces mango purée

2 ounces sugar

2 ounces egg whites

# COFFEE PANNA COTTA WITH MANGO YOLK

THIS IS PROBABLY THE ALL-TIME NUMBER 1 DESSERT AT UCHI. PEOPLE LOSE THEIR MINDS OVER THIS. VISUALLY, THEY CAN'T GET OVER HOW BEAUTIFUL IT IS, AND THE FLAVORS AND TEXTURES JUST MAKE THE EXPERIENCE OF IT EVEN BETTER. I JUST WANTED TO TRY TO DO A DESSERT THAT HAD A YOLK LIKE AN EGG. AND THE TEXTURE OF THE PANNA COTTA WITH THE CRUNCHY COFFEE SOIL...IT'S JUST ONE OF THE BEST DESSERTS EVER.

**FOR THE COFFEE MILK:** Bring milk and coffee beans to a boil in small saucepan. Remove from heat and let steep overnight. Reserve for later use in recipe.

**FOR THE MANGO YOLK:** Combine ingredients in a small saucepan. Bring to a boil and turn off heat. Pour into hemisphere molds and freeze for later use. (These molds can be purchased online.)

**FOR THE COFFEE PANNA COTTA:** Bloom gelatin in ice water. Bring coffee milk, salt, and sugar to boiling point in medium saucepan. Remove from heat and add bloomed gelatin. Mix well using a hand-held blender to combine and let cool to room temperature. Whip heavy cream to soft peaks in a separate bowl. Quickly whisk the coffee milk mixture with whipped cream. Divide cream and coffee mixture into 6 hemisphere molds. Push frozen mango yolks into center of filled molds. Carefully center the yolks. If they are too high they will leak out, and if they are too low they will show through the top. Place in freezer to set, about 3 hours. When the panna cottas are frozen solid, remove from molds and place on parchment-lined sheet tray. Use individual parchment sheets under each panna cotta. Refrigerate to let thaw before serving, about 4 hours.

**FOR THE COFFEE SOIL:** Preheat oven to 350° F. In food processor, grind together all ingredients except butter. Grind into fine crumbs. Add melted butter to ground mixture. Mix well with hands. Spread mixture onto parchment-lined full sheet tray. Bake for 10 to 12 minutes. Once cooled, crush soil and store in an airtight container.

**FOR THE WHITE CHOCOLATE SORBET:** Bring first 3 ingredients to a boil. Remove from heat and add white chocolate. Mix well with hand-held blender. Let cool, and spin in ice cream machine according to manufacturer's directions.

**FOR THE MANGO PAPER:** Combine all ingredients and mix well with hand-held blender. Spread on sheet tray and dry overnight in a gas oven with the pilot light on or in an electric oven set to 100° F.

**ASSEMBLY:** To serve, cover half of a round plate with coffee soil. Place coffee panna cotta next to soil. Place a scoop of white chocolate sorbet onto mound of coffee soil. Finish with mango paper.

GRAPEFRUIT SORBET

**GRAPEFRUIT SORBET**

48 ounces grapefruit juice

16 ounces glucose syrup

¼ ounce sugar

½ ounce stabilizer

½ ounce salt

**AVOCADO PURÉE**

2 avocados

4 ounces simple syrup

Juice of 1 lime

Kosher salt to taste

Pinch of citric acid

**FENNEL CONFIT**

4 ounces fennel

4 ounces water

3 ounces sugar

1 ounce trimoline

Kosher salt to taste

Juice of ½ lemon

**FENNEL CHIP**

1 fennel bulb

2 ounces simple syrup

**GARNISH**

Fresh grapefruit slices

Drizzle olive oil

Pinch maldon salt

A few fennel fronds

# GRAPEFRUIT SORBET
## *AVOCADO PURÉE, FENNEL CONFIT*

I USED TO HATE GRAPEFRUIT. ONLY RECENTLY HAVE I COME TO LIKE IT. I HAD IT ONCE AS A SORBET WITH SOME BLACK HAWAIIAN SALT ON IT, AND I JUST COULDN'T GET ENOUGH OF IT. SO PHILIP SPEER AND I STARTED PLAYING WITH OTHER FLAVORS THAT GO WELL WITH GRAPE-FRUIT, AND IT TURNED OUT AVOCADO AND FENNEL WERE PERFECT. IT'S BEAUTIFUL, AND IT'S A REALLY REFRESHING DESSERT.

**FOR GRAPEFRUIT SORBET:** Combine all ingredients and freeze in an ice cream machine, according to manufacturer's directions. Reserve in freezer.

**FOR THE AVOCADO PURÉE:** Peel and pit avocados. In a blender, combine avocados, simple syrup, and lime juice. Blend on medium until smooth. Add kosher salt and citric acid. Continue to blend until the purée is of uniform texture. Reserve in the refrigerator, covered.

**FOR THE FENNEL CONFIT:** With a sharp knife, brunoise cut (¹⁄₁₆-inch dice) the fennel and reserve. In a small saucepan, combine water, sugar, and trimoline, and bring to a boil. Let mixture cook until it is reduced by about ¼. Add fennel and immediately remove from heat. The residual heat will cook the fennel. Season with salt and add lemon juice. Reserve in refrigerator.

**FOR THE FENNEL CHIP:** Slice fennel bulb, paper thin, on a mandolin. Soak slices in the simple syrup, and place on a silicon baking mat in a dehydrator overnight or in a gas oven with the pilot light on or in an electric oven set to 100° F.

**ASSEMBLY:** On a cold plate, slice a peeled grapefruit into paper thin slices, cutting with the grain. Arrange these slices across the plate, similar to a carpaccio plate. Place three scoops of sorbet across the plate on top of the grapefruit. Add large dollops of avocado purée between sorbet scoops. Place small spoonfuls of fennel confit between the avocado purée. Drizzle olive oil across the grapefruit and finish the plate with fennel chips, maldon salt, and a few fennel fronds. Serve immediately.

# HAZELNUT SORBET

## *HAZELNUT MOUSSE, HAZELNUT BUTTER, HAZELNUT CRUNCH, FLEUR DE SEL*

I HAD AN OBSESSION WITH HAZELNUTS FOR A LITTLE WHILE, AND WHEN I FIXATE ON A FLAVOR, I HAVE TO WORK WITH IT IN EVERY WAY I CAN THINK OF. SO, OF COURSE, WE DID A DESSERT. WE TOOK THIS COMPONENT AND USED IT FOUR WAYS. WE DID EVERYTHING WE COULD TO SHOWCASE HOW GREAT THE FLAVORS CAN BE WHEN YOU USE THE HAZELNUT IN DIFFERENT WAYS.

**FOR THE HAZELNUT SORBET:** Combine all ingredients and cook over low heat for 15 minutes. Purée all contents in a blender and strain through a fine mesh sieve. Use a ladle to push the liquid through. Cool over an ice bath and spin in an ice cream machine according to manufacturer's instructions.

**FOR THE HAZELNUT BUTTER:** Place all ingredients into food processor and blend well until paste achieves texture of peanut butter. With a piping bag, pipe 3-inch strips of the hazelnut butter and freeze for the centers of the mousse, about 4 hours.

**FOR THE HAZELNUT MOUSSE:** Bloom gelatin in ice water for 5 minutes. Remove and squeeze out excess water. In a medium-sized sauce pot, cook the milk, sugar, salt, and hazelnuts for 15 minutes over low heat. Purée in a blender, while still hot, and strain with a fine mesh sieve. About 6 ounces of liquid should result. While the hazelnut milk is still hot, add bloomed gelatin and let cool to room temperature, stirring frequently. Whip the cream to stiff peaks and fold the room-temperature hazelnut milk into the cream to create a mousse. Pipe mousse into cylinder molds lined with acetate strips, and place frozen hazelnut butter into the middle of the mousse. Freeze the mousse to set and remove from mold when ready for cutting. Slice the mousse into 4 slices, running

across the butter center. Reserve in refrigerator to soften up for use.

**FOR THE HAZELNUT CRUNCH:** Combine the sugar and water in a medium pot and bring to a boil. Add the hazelnuts to the boiling water and cook for 15 minutes over medium-low heat. Heat a pan with vegetable oil for frying to 325º F. Remove hazelnuts from the syrup and fry until golden brown. Remove from frying oil and toss in 1 part sugar to 1 part salt mixture. In a food processor grind candied hazelnuts to a pebble size. Reserve in airtight container.

**FOR THE SEA SALT FOAM:** Combine water, sugar, and salt in a small sauce pot and bring to a boil. Remove from heat and add a pinch of soy lecithin. With a handheld blender, blend the mixture, trying to incorporate as much air as possible. Let the mixture sit for 1 minute and a foam will collect at the top.

**ASSEMBLY:** Place two large spoonfuls of hazelnut crunch across a rectangular plate. Arrange the 4 slices of the hazelnut mousse across the crunch. Spoon the foam across the mousse, and finish with a quenelle of the sorbet next to the mousse, on top of the crunch. Serve immediately.

### HAZELNUT SORBET

8 ounces roasted hazelnuts

16 ounces water

4 ounces sugar

2 ounces corn syrup

¼ ounce kosher salt

### HAZELNUT BUTTER

16 ounces roasted hazelnuts

1 ounce hazelnut oil

4 ounces sugar

1 ounce kosher salt

### HAZELNUT MOUSSE

2 sheets gelatin

Ice water

16 ounces milk

4 ounces sugar

¼ ounce kosher salt

8 ounces roasted hazelnuts

12 ounces heavy
    whipping cream

### HAZELNUT CRUNCH

8 ounces sugar

8 ounces water

8 ounces hazelnuts

Vegetable oil for frying,
    enough to coat the pan

Kosher salt and sugar
    to toss crunch

### SEA SALT FOAM

6 ounces water

2 ounces sugar

1 ounce fleur de sel

1 pinch of soy lecithin

# ICED MILK SHERBET
## *FRIED MILK, SOFT CHOCOLATE MILK,*
## *TOASTED MILK POWDER*

THIS IS OUR TAKE ON MILK IN FOUR DIFFERENT WAYS: ICED MILK, FRIED MILK, CHOCOLATE MILK, TOASTED MILK. IT WAS SOMETHING PHILIP CAME UP WITH FROM A TECHNIQUE HE HAD READ ABOUT. IT'S TAKING CREAM AND FREEZING IT, THEN FRYING IT, ALMOST LIKE FRIED ICE CREAM. SO WE DID AN ICED-MILK SHERBET FOR A CLEAN ADDITION AND THEN THE CHOCOLATE MILK TUILE WITH TOASTED MILK, WHICH WE MADE INTO A "SOIL" AT THE BOTTOM OF THE PLATE. IT'S WONDERFUL.

**FOR THE ICED MILK SHERBET:** Combine sugar, salt, and stabilizer in a bowl. In a large sauce pot, combine milk and corn syrup and slowly add the sugar mixture. Mix well to incorporate. Heat over medium heat until sugar has dissolved and the mixture is a uniform consistency. Cool over an ice bath. Freeze in ice cream machine according to manufacturer's instructions.

**FOR THE CHOCOLATE OIL:** Slowly melt the chocolate with the oil over a double boiler on low heat. Stir in the cocoa powder and mix well to combine. Reserve chocolate oil at room temperature for later use.

**FOR THE CHOCOLATE MILK TUILE:** Melt butter and place into a food processor. Add all other ingredients and combine well. Chill batter in the refrigerator. Spread on a silicon baking mat and bake at 325° F for 8 to 10 minutes. Once cooled, break into large pieces and reserve.

**FOR THE FRIED MILK:** In a medium-sized saucepan, combine cream and vanilla bean and bring to the boiling point on high heat. In a large bowl whisk together sugar, salt, and cornstarch. Add eggs and yolk, and whisk well to incorporate evenly. Slowly temper vanilla-infused cream *(continued on page 226 . . .)*

*(continued on page 226 . . .)*

### FRIED MILK

16 ounces cream

1 vanilla bean, split

4 ounces sugar

Kosher salt to taste

1 ounce cornstarch

2 whole eggs

1 egg yolk

### BREADING

8 ounces crispy rice cereal

8 eggs, mixed well

8 ounces all-purpose flour

Oil for deep frying

### ICED MILK SHERBET

4 ounces sugar

Pinch of salt

¾ ounce stabilizer

32 ounces milk

6 ounces corn syrup

### CHOCOLATE OIL

3½ ounces dark chocolate

3½ ounces vegetable oil

½ ounce cocoa powder

### CHOCOLATE MILK TUILE

5 ounces butter

8 ounces sugar

12 ounces cocoa powder

Kosher salt to taste

¼ ounce vanilla extract

4 egg whites

### SOFT CHOCOLATE MILK

1½ sheets gelatin

Ice water

3 ounces 70 percent
   Valrhona chocolate

3½ ounces milk

Kosher salt to taste

5½ ounces cream

### TOASTED MILK POWDER

2 ounces dehydrated milk

2 ounces ground crispy
   rice cereal

*(. . . Iced Milk Sherbet continued)*

into egg mixture, scraping vanilla beans into the mixture, and mix well. Return mixture to pan and cook over medium heat until mixture has thickened. Consistency should be similar to pudding. Remove from heat and cool in an ice bath. Pour cream onto a parchment-lined sheet tray and freeze to set completely, at least 4 hours. Remove from freezer and cut into 1-inch cubes. Return cubes to the freezer and reserve for breading.

**FOR THE BREADING:** Finely grind crispy rice cereal in food processor. Place ground cereal, beaten eggs, and flour in their own small bowls. Remove frozen milk cubes from the freezer and coat evenly with flour. Dip flour-coated cubes into the bowl of eggs and coat evenly. Finally, coat the cubes in the cereal. Return to freezer to solidify. To fry, heat oil to 325° F in a pan. Submerge cubes and fry until breading is golden brown and crispy.

**FOR THE SOFT CHOCOLATE MILK:** Bloom sheets of gelatin in ice water for 5 minutes. Remove and squeeze out extra moisture. Melt chocolate over a double boiler. In a medium saucepan, heat milk and salt over medium heat and pour over melted chocolate. Add bloomed gelatin and mix well, being careful not to incorporate too much air. Whip cream to soft peaks. When chocolate and milk mixture has cooled to room temperature, fold in the whipped cream. Pipe mixture into 6 miniature terrine molds and freeze to make unmolding easier. Reserve in refrigerator for later use.

**FOR THE TOASTED MILK POWDER:** Preheat oven to 300° F. In a medium sheet pan, toast the dehydrated milk until golden brown. Mix with the ground cereal, and reserve in an airtight container until needed.

**ASSEMBLY:** Place a spoonful of the toasted milk powder along the plate in a row. Place soft chocolate milk terrine in the center of the plate. Add 3 fried milks on either side of the plate. Place 2 scoops of milk sherbet in between the fried milks. Pool the chocolate oil along the plate, in between the toasted milk powder. Finish the plate with 2 chocolate milk tuiles.

# JIZAKE CRÈME CARAMEL
## *BROWN BUTTER SORBET, GINGER CONSOMMÉ*

ZAKE IS "SHORT" FOR SAKE. WHEN THINGS GO TOGETHER WITH SAKE, YOU CHANGE THE "S" TO A "Z." SO "JIZAKE" MEANS "OF SAKE." JIZAKE IS UNFILTERED AND MILKY. IT'S A NATURAL COMPONENT, ALMOST LIKE COCONUT WATER, AND YOU CAN DO SO MUCH WITH IT. WE'VE PAIRED IT WITH THE BROWN BUTTER SORBET, WHICH IS ONE OF OUR BEST CREATIONS. I ONCE HAD A DINNER DISH WITH A BROWN BUTTER SAUCE THAT HAD THE BEST FLAVOR, AND I BECAME OBSESSED WITH MAKING A SORBET WITH IT. AT FIRST, PHILIP SPEER SAID IT WAS IMPOSSIBLE BECAUSE OF THE BUTTER FATS, BUT HE NAILED IT. WE PUT THAT WITH A GINGER CONSOMMÉ AND THE JIZAKE CARAMEL, AND IT WAS A HUGE HIT.

*FOR THE JIZAKE CRÈME CARAMEL:* Preheat oven to 300° F. In a small saucepan, heat sake over medium-high heat and reduce by ¾ volume. Bloom gelatin in ice water for at least 5 minutes or until soft. Squeeze out excess moisture. In a medium pan, bring cream and milk to a boil. At boiling point, add reduced sake and bloomed gelatin and whisk together, mixing well. In a separate bowl, combine 2 ounces of sugar, egg, and egg yolks and whisk well to combine. While sake mixture is still hot, slowly temper into egg and sugar mixture. Mix well and add salt. Strain through chinois and reserve. Place 5 ounces of sugar in small sauce pot and add water. Let water soak into sugar and place on stove over medium heat. Cook sugar and water to caramelize to an amber color. It should reach about 320° F. Remove from heat and use a ladle to coat the bottom of 4 ramekins with caramelized sugar. Once cooled, fill each ramekin with crème mixture. Place filled ramekins in a large high-sided pan and fill pan with water, about ⅔ of the way up the sides of ramekins. Bake 25 to 35 minutes, gently rotating pan in the oven at the halfway point. Remove from oven when custards have a uniform jiggle. Store in refrigerator.

*FOR THE BROWN BUTTER SORBET:* Place butter into a small sauce pot. Turn heat on high. When butter starts melting and bubbling, lower heat to medium. Cook butter until the solids start to brown. Continue cooking until solids are almost black. At this point, add sugar quickly, followed by water. Continue to cook until near boiling point and add corn syrup. Remove from heat and set in an ice bath. When all of the butter has solidified and separated to the top of the pot, remove solidified butter and strain remaining liquid through a fat filter into an ice cream container. Spin in an ice cream machine according to manufacturer's instructions.
*(continued on page 231...)*

**JIZAKE CRÈME CARMEL**

4 ounces Nigori sake

1 sheet gelatin

Ice water

5 ounces cream

7 ounces milk

7 ounces sugar

1 whole egg

2 egg yolks

Kosher salt

2 ounces water

**BROWN BUTTER SORBET**

8 ounces butter

8 ounces sugar

32 ounces water

3 ounces light corn syrup

Ice bath

**ALMOND GLASS**

1 ounce almond slices

½ ounce isomalt powder*

*Isomalt powder can be found at any baking supply store.

**GINGER CONSOMMÉ**

1 ounce fresh ginger, peeled

4 ounces water

2 ounces sugar

Kosher salt to taste

*(. . . Jizake Crème Caramel continued)*

**FOR THE ALMOND GLASS:** Preheat oven to 325° F. Spread almonds onto a baking sheet lined with a silicon baking mat or parchment paper. Sprinkle the powdered isomalt evenly over the sliced almonds and bake until the almonds have browned and the isomalt has completely melted, 10 to 12 minutes. Peel the mat or paper from the almonds and reserve the almond glass in an airtight container until needed.

**FOR THE GINGER CONSOMMÉ:** Chop peeled ginger into ¼-inch slices and mix with water, sugar, and salt in a small sauce pot. Bring to a boil, then remove from heat. Strain the ginger and reserve the consommé in the refrigerator until needed.

**ASSEMBLY:** Run a small knife around each ramekin to loosen the crème caramel from the edges. Flip the ramekins over so the crème caramel falls out. Place onto a round, shallow bowl. Place ½ ounce of the almond glass in the bowl next to the crème caramel. Place a quenelle of sorbet onto the almond glass. Finish the dish with 2 ounces ginger consommé and a bit more almond glass for garnish.

# LEMON GELATO
## *WITH BEET AND SICILIAN PISTACHIO*

WE USE LEMON IN SO MANY THINGS ON THE UCHI MENU. IT'S A PERFECT ACID. LEMON DESSERTS ARE POPULAR AT EVERY RESTAURANT, AND WE WANTED TO HAVE ONE OF OUR OWN. WE PLAYED WITH A NUMBER OF VARIATIONS, BUT THIS IS ONE OF MY FAVORITES. I LOVE THE COLORS WITH THE BEETS AND THE TEXTURE OF THE PISTACHIO. IT'S A GREAT BALANCE OF INGREDIENTS.

### GOLDEN BEET PURÉE

1 pound golden beets

Kosher salt

1 ounce water

2 ounces simple syrup

¼ teaspoon white vinegar

1½ ounces melted butter

### LEMON GELATO

1 ounce lemon zest

30 ounces milk

7 ounces sugar

¼ ounce salt

¼ ounce sorbet stabilizer

3 ounces glucose

1 vanilla bean, split
    and scraped

9 ounces heavy cream

### PISTACHIO CRUMBLE

40 ounces Sicilian
    pistachios

16 ounces flour

1 tablespoon salt

16 ounces sugar

8 ounces butter

### WHITE BALSAMIC REDUCTION

8 ounces white balsamic
    vinegar

1 ounce sugar

### CURED LEMON ZEST

2 whole lemons

8 ounces water

8 ounces sugar

1 ounce kosher salt

Pinch of fresh ground
    juniper

### BEET GLASS

1 large golden beet

2 egg whites

2 ounces sugar

2 ounces water

### GARNISH

Toasted Sicilian pistachios

**FOR THE GOLDEN BEET PURÉE:** Preheat oven to 350° F and rinse beets thoroughly. Season liberally with kosher salt and wrap wet beets in aluminum foil. Roast until fork tender, about 2½ hours. When beets have cooled enough to handle, peel off the skin. It should fall off very easily. Chop the beets into small uniform pieces, about ¼ inch in size. Place into a blender and pulse to start the blending process. Use water and simple syrup to help loosen up the purée. Add the vinegar and season to taste with a bit more salt. Finish purée by gently streaming melted butter into purée to emulsify and give it a sheen and smooth consistency. Reserve the purée at room temperature for later use.

**FOR THE LEMON GELATO:** In a large pot, combine all ingredients except cream. Bring to a boil, then remove from heat and let steep for at least 4 hours or overnight. Once mixture has cooled to at least 50° F, add heavy cream and mix well. Strain mixture and freeze in ice cream machine according to manufacturer's instructions.

**FOR THE PISTACHIO CRUMBLE:** Preheat oven to 350° F. In a food processor, grind Sicilian pistachios to a fine consistency, but not paste-like. Remove pistachios from blender and measure out 32 ounces. In the same food processor, blend flour, salt, and sugar until well combined. Cut butter into small cubes and pulse into the mixture until it is a sandy consistency. Add half of the ground pistachio back into the butter and flour mixture, and pulse until well combined. Mix remaining pistachio flour into the dough by hand and spread evenly over a baking sheet. Bake 10 to 12 minutes or until edges begin to get golden. Once crumble has cooled, break apart with hands and reserve at room temperature in an airtight container until needed.

**FOR THE WHITE BALSAMIC REDUCTION:** Over low heat, reduce white balsamic vinegar by ¾ volume. Add sugar and continue to cook until it has dissolved. Remove from heat and reserve at room temperature.

(continued on page 235 . . .)

*(. . . Lemon Gelato continued)*

**FOR THE CURED LEMON ZEST:** With a potato peeler, peel lemon zest from the rind of the lemon. Keep the zest pieces large. In a medium-sized sauce pot, bring about 32 ounces of water to a boil. Blanch zest in the boiling water and repeat the process 5 times, with new water each time. In a separate sauce pot, combine 8 ounces of water with 6 ounces of sugar and bring to a boil. Place the blanched zest into the boiling mixture. Let the zest cook over low heat 15 to 20 minutes. The zest should start becoming translucent. Combine 2 ounces of sugar, kosher salt, and ground juniper in a small bowl. Mix well and pour into a plastic container. Add zest and cure in mixture for at least 2 hours. Once you are ready to use the zest, slice very thin.

**FOR THE BEET GLASS:** Preheat oven to 300° F and roast beet until fork-tender, about 2 hours. Remove skin and chop beet into small uniform pieces. Place into a blender with remaining ingredients. Blend until very smooth. On a piece of acetate, spread the beet mixture over a dehydrator rack in a paper-thin layer. Dehydrate overnight. If you do not have a dehydrator, place overnight in a gas oven with the pilot light on or in an electric oven set to 100° F.

**ASSEMBLY:** Place spoonful, or about 2 ounces, of the beet purée in the bottom of a shallow bowl, spreading with swipe of the spoon on bowl's surface. Lay 2 ounces of pistachio crumble next to the purée. Place two quenelles of lemon gelato on top of the crumble. Add 6 to 10 toasted Sicilian pistachios to the dessert. Drizzle a bit of white balsamic reduction next to the gelato, over the beet purée. Finish with a few shards of beet glass and a couple pieces of cured lemon zest.

# MASCARPONE SPHERE
## WITH CURED STRAWBERRY, PEA SORBET AND MINT CHIPS

THIS IS ONE OF MY THREE FAVORITE DESSERTS THAT WE'VE MADE. WE CURE STRAWBERRIES AND COMPRESS THEM. WITH THE MASCARPONE CREAM, FRESH MINT, AND PEA SORBET, EVERYTHING JUST FITS. THE COMBINATION IS FANTASTIC, WITH A NUMBER OF DIFFERENT TEXTURES. THE FLAVORS JUST SORT OF BURST.

**FOR THE MASCARPONE SPHERE:** Bloom gelatin in ice water for 5 minutes or until soft. Remove and squeeze out excess moisture. Beat egg yolks in medium bowl. In a small saucepan, combine cream, sugar, and salt. Bring to a boil, then remove from heat. Slowly temper hot mixture into egg yolks. Add gelatin to hot mixture. Mix well and let cool to room temperature. Combine with mascarpone cheese, not incorporating any air into the mixture. When all ingredients are consistently combined, strain through chinois several times to remove any air bubbles. Pour into spherical mold and refrigerate to set, then place in freezer for 4 hours. Remove spheres from molds and leave in freezer until at least 4 hours before service.

**FOR PEA SHORTBREAD:** Preheat oven to 300° F. To make pea flour, grind dehydrated peas in a spice grinder until flour-like. Mix together flour, pea flour, sugar, and salt. Cut in cold butter and mix well. Bake 7 to 10 minutes. Crumble into a thick, coarse powder, and reserve for later use.

**FOR THE MINT CHIPS:** Chop cold cream cheese into small chunks. Place egg whites, salt, and sugar into blender and start mixing on low speed. Add chunks of cheese, one at a time, into blender while gradually increasing speed. Scrape down sides of blender with a rubber spatula and continue to mix until well incorporated. Add mint extract and mix well. Spread batter thinly onto acetate with an offset spatula. (Batter should be about the width of construction paper.) Place in dehydrator for at least 8 hours, or overnight in a gas oven with the pilot light on or in an electric oven set to 100° F. Break the hardened mint paper into larger chips. Store in an airtight plastic container with silica pearls.

**FOR THE CURED STRAWBERRIES:** Mix salt and sugar together in a mixing bowl. Add strawberries and coat well with cure. Place coated strawberries into vacuum bag and seal at 100 percent. Leave filled bag in refrigerator overnight. To use, slice into ⅛-inch rounds.

**FOR THE SWEET PEA SORBET:** Bring a large pot of water to a boil. Cook peas until they turn bright green, 1 to 3 minutes. Drain, immediately submerge in cold water, and drain again. Transfer half of the peas and half of the mint to a blender and purée. Pass the purée through a food mill into a large bowl. Purée the remaining peas and remaining mint, and strain into the same bowl. Stir in water and strain the mixture through food mill or fine-mesh sieve into a large pitcher. Mix in corn syrup and salt. Spin in an ice cream machine according to manufacturer's instructions.

**ASSEMBLY:** Place a small pile of pea shortbread powder on the bottom of a shallow bowl, with a mascarpone sphere on top. Place a large quenelle of the pea sorbet next to the sphere. Add a few cured strawberries around the sphere, leaving some juice in the bowl. Finish with mint chips and serve immediately.

---

### MASCARPONE SPHERE

3 sheets gelatin

Ice water

2 egg yolks

10 ounces heavy cream

3 ounces sugar

Kosher salt

8 ounces mascarpone cheese

### PEA SHORTBREAD

2 ounces dehydrated peas* for pea flour

1 ounces all-purpose flour

1 ounce sugar

Kosher salt to taste

1 ounce butter, very cold

*You can buy dehydrated peas at specialty food markets.

### MINT CHIPS

2 ounces cream cheese

2 egg whites

Kosher salt to taste

2 cups sugar

2 drops peppermint extract

### CURED STRAWBERRIES

3 ounces salt

6 ounces sugar

8 ounces strawberries

### SWEET PEA SORBET

14 ounces fresh peas

1 ounce fresh mint leaves, divided

2 ounces water

2½ ounces corn syrup

Kosher salt to taste

**PEANUT BUTTER SEMIFREDDO**

12 ounces heavy whipping cream

¼ teaspoon salt

¾ tablespoon vanilla extract

4 ounces cream cheese, at room temperature

4 ounces creamy peanut butter

4 ounces sugar

**GOLDEN RAISIN PURÉE**

10 ounces golden raisins

4 ounces water

4 ounces sake

4 ounces mirin

½ teaspoon salt

**APPLE MISO SORBET**

8 ounces unpeeled Fuji apple

2 ounces miso paste

16 ounces simple syrup

4 ounces water

1 teaspoon salt

**GARNISH**

Ground peanut brittle

Dehydrated apple slices

# PEANUT BUTTER SEMIFREDDO
## *WITH APPLE MISO SORBET AND GOLDEN RAISIN PURÉE*

THIS WAS AN IDEA I HAD EARLY ON AT THE RESTAURANT. I LOVE PEANUT BUTTER AND APPLES TOGETHER. WE STARTED PLAYING WITH MISO FOR OUR DESSERTS, AND WE FELT PEANUT BUTTER COULD BE A PERFECT COMBINATION FOR THIS, FOR THE SAVORY ASPECT AND THE TEXTURE. IT'S ONE OF THE MORE RICH DESSERTS WE HAVE AND ONE OF THE MOST POPULAR AT THE RESTAURANT.

***FOR THE PEANUT BUTTER SEMIFREDDO:*** Whip cold heavy cream, salt, and vanilla to soft peaks, chill, and reserve. In mixer, combine cream cheese, peanut butter, and sugar. Mix well, until mixture is smooth. Add half of reserved whipped cream. Mix well, being careful not to overmix. Transfer into large mixing bowl. Gently fold in remaining whipped cream. Pour mixture into plastic wrap-lined terrine mold. Freeze a minimum of 4 hours.

***FOR THE GOLDEN RAISIN PURÉE:*** Combine all ingredients in small saucepan. Bring to a boil and turn off heat. Let raisins sit in the pan for 30 minutes to rehydrate. Purée all ingredients in blender until smooth. Refrigerate in a squeeze bottle for service. Reserve leftover in an airtight container.

***FOR THE APPLE MISO SORBET:*** In blender, purée Fuji apples, and combine with miso paste. Add simple syrup, water, and salt. Chill mixture and freeze in ice cream machine according to manufacturer's directions.

***ASSEMBLY:*** Half an hour before serving time, remove terrine from freezer. With a hot knife, slice desired serving sizes, about ¾ inch thick. Place slice on a serving plate and refrigerate to raise temperature. The goal is to have a partially frozen center with a creamy soft outside. When ready for serving, scoop a liberal serving of apple miso sorbet next to the semifreddo and finish with golden raisin purée. At Uchi, we also garnish with ground peanut brittle and dehydrated apple slices, "ringo crisps."

# POLENTA CUSTARD

## *WITH CORN SORBET, CORN MILK, AND CORN BREAD TUILE*

I LOVE PICKING A COLOR FOR A DESSERT AND HAVING EVERY COMPONENT OF THE DISH FIT THAT SCHEME. FOR THIS DISH, WE CHOSE YELLOW. IT WAS A PLAY ON CORN, WITH A SORBET MADE FROM SWEET CORN JUICE, A CUSTARD WITH POLENTA FOR A NICE TEXTURE, A TUILE (OUR TAKE ON CORN BREAD), AND A LEMON GEL FOR A COMPLEMENTARY FLAVOR IN THE YELLOW SCHEME. IT'S SWEET, SALTY, COLD. I LIKE USING SORBET IN OUR DESSERTS. IT ADDS A LIGHT, CRISP ELEMENT, WHICH IS INDICATIVE OF UCHI FOOD.

**POLENTA CUSTARD**

1 ounce polenta

8 ounces cream

2 ounces sugar

1 vanilla bean, split

Kosher salt to taste

3 egg yolks

¼ ounce milk

**CORN SORBET**

2 pounds fresh corn kernels

Quantity of water for corn milk

2 ounces sugar

¼ ounce white vinegar

2 ounces glucose syrup

¼ ounce kosher salt

**CORN BREAD TUILE**

1 ounce polenta

4 ounces milk

¼ ounce butter

½ ounce sugar

Kosher salt to taste

**LEMON FLUID GEL**

⅛ ounce agar agar

8 ounces water

4 ounces sugar

2 ounces lemon juice

Salt to taste

**CORN MILK**

32 ounces corn juice

5 ounces sugar

4 ounces butter

kosher salt to taste

*FOR THE POLENTA CUSTARD:* Preheat oven to 300° F. Combine polenta, cream, 1 ounce sugar, vanilla beans, and salt in a medium saucepan. Bring to a boil and then turn heat down and let simmer. Frequently stir until polenta is fully cooked, about 15 minutes. Taste polenta and make sure bitterness has gone away. If not, continue to cook. In a separate bowl, whisk together 1 ounce sugar and egg yolks. Slowly temper hot polenta into mixture. Add milk to slightly loosen up batter. Pour into desired molds and bake in a water bath for about 25 minutes, or until custard has a uniform jiggle. Refrigerate to set. If needed, after custard has set, freeze to make cutting easier.

*FOR THE CORN SORBET:* Purée corn kernels with a bit of water and pass through a fine mesh sieve. Combine 8 ounces of this corn milk with remaining ingredients over low heat. Chill over an ice bath and freeze in ice cream maker according to manufacturer's instructions. Reserve excess corn milk for later use.

*FOR THE CORN MILK:* Combine ingredients and cook over medium heat, stirring constantly. The corn milk will thicken with the natural starch in the corn. Once thick, remove from heat and reserve for later use.

*FOR THE CORN BREAD TUILE:* Preheat oven to 300° F. Combine ingredients in a small saucepan and cook over medium heat. Once polenta is fully cooked, spread on a silicon baking mat in paper-thin 3-inch circles. Bake until the tuiles are golden brown, 8 to 10 minutes. Reserve in an airtight container for later use.

*FOR THE LEMON FLUID GEL:* In a medium-sized saucepan, sprinkle the agar agar on top of the water and let sit for 5 minutes to bloom. Add the sugar to mixture and place over medium-high heat. Stirring constantly, bring the mixture to a boil and cook for one minute. Continue to stir vigorously. Remove from heat and add the lemon juice and salt. Pour into a plastic container and refrigerate to set, about 1 hour. Once the mixture has set, place into a blender on high until the lemon gel reaches a fluid consistency. Remove from blender and refrigerate until ready for use.

*ASSEMBLY:* Place 1 ounce of corn milk along the bottom of a shallow bowl. Place dots of the lemon gel around the corn milk. Place the polenta custard on top of the corn milk. Lay a quenelle of corn sorbet on top of the polenta custard. Finish the plate with a piece of corn bread tuile.

# PINE NEEDLE SORBET

## *WITH ORANGE GLACÉ, CANDIED PINE NUT, AND ORANGE TUILE*

**WE ONCE HAD A PASTRY APPRENTICE FROM MINNESOTA WHO CAME UP WITH THE IDEA TO USE PINE NEEDLES IN A SORBET. WE LOVE HOW IT TURNED OUT; IT HAS SORT OF A GIN FLAVOR TO IT. THE DISH HAS A NICE CRUNCH FROM THE PINE NUT CANDY, AND THE ORANGE GLACÉ PULLS IT TOGETHER WITH THE SWEETNESS.**

### PINE NEEDLE SORBET

2 ounces pine needles

Ice water bath

2 ounces sugar

1 ounce glucose

8 ounces water

Kosher salt to taste

### ORANGE GLACÉ

2 gelatin sheets

Ice water

4 ounces milk

2 ounces sugar

4 oranges

10 ounces heavy cream

Kosher salt to taste

### CANDIED PINE NUT

Soybean oil, enough to
    coat a pan for frying
    pine nuts

5 ounces sugar

4 ounces water

4 ounces pine nuts

Kosher salt to taste

### ORANGE TUILE

2½ ounces melted butter

4 ounces sugar

1 ounce fresh orange juice

Zest of 1 orange

Pinch of kosher salt

2 ounces flour

**FOR THE PINE NEEDLE SORBET:** Blanch the pine needles in boiling water for 5 seconds. Remove and immediately shock in an ice water bath. In a medium sauce pot, combine sugar, glucose, water, and salt and bring to a boil, stirring often. Remove from stove and cool in a bowl over ice bath. Once the sorbet base is cold, blend the liquid with the pine needles in a blender. Do not let the liquid get too hot from blending or your base will brown. Strain through a fine mesh sieve and let cool. Reserve pulp for pine needle powder. Reserve 2 ounces of the sorbet base for the pine needle syrup. Spin in sorbet machine according to manufacturer's directions.

**FOR THE ORANGE GLACÉ:** Bloom sheets of gelatin in ice water for 5 minutes, or until gelatin sheets are soft and pliable. Remove and squeeze out excess water. In a small sauce pot heat together milk and sugar until heated through and sugar has dissolved. Be careful not to scald the milk. While milk is heating, zest the oranges, squeeze the juice in with the zest, and add to heated milk. Add bloomed gelatin while mixture is still hot and mix well to combine. In a separate bowl, whip the cream to stiff peaks and reserve. Once the milk mixture reaches room temperature, gently fold it into the whipped cream. Fill desired molds with the mixture and freeze. When ready to serve, unmold the glacé and let it sit in the refrigerator for about 30 minutes to soften.

**FOR THE CANDIED PINE NUTS:** Heat a medium pan to 325° F and add soybean oil. Combine 4 ounces of sugar with water in a separate medium pan and bring to a boil. Add pine nuts and cook for 15 minutes over medium-low heat. Remove the pine nuts from the syrup and fry until golden. Remove from oil and toss in remaining sugar and salt. Reserve candied pine nuts in an airtight container.

**FOR THE ORANGE TUILE:** Combine all ingredients in a food processor. Refrigerate tuile batter for 1 hour. Preheat oven to 325° F. Place a teaspoon-sized ball of batter on a silicone baking mat and bake 8 to 10 minutes or until tuile has spread and is a dark golden brown. Bake tuiles one at a time. Remove tuile from mat while it is still warm. Store tuiles in an airtight container until ready for use.

**FOR THE PINE NEEDLE POWDER:** Dehydrate the reserved pine needle pulp overnight in a dehydrator, or place overnight in a gas oven with the pilot light on or in an electric oven set to 100° F. Grind in a spice grinder and reserve.

**FOR THE PINE NEEDLE SYRUP:** Reduce the reserved sorbet base by about ½ in a small sauce pot over very low heat.

**ASSEMBLY:** Place the orange glacé in a shallow bowl with a spoonful of candied pine nuts next to it. Place a quenelle of pine sorbet on top of the pine nuts. Sprinkle some of the pine needle powder next to the sorbet. Garnish with the pine syrup and an orange tuile. Finish with a pinch of orange zest on the sorbet.

ROASTED TOMATO SORBET

# ROASTED TOMATO SORBET
## CHERUB TOMATO CONFIT, CHEVRE FONDANT

**TOMATOES IN A DESSERT ARE A BIT OF A DEPARTURE FOR MOST PEOPLE. ROASTING THE TOMATOES FOR THE SORBET REALLY BRINGS OUT A PERFECT SWEETNESS. IT'S A DESSERT THAT'S UNEXPECTED BUT REALLY GOOD.**

**GOAT CHEESE FONDANT**

2 sheets gelatin

Ice water

6 ounces cream

4 ounces sugar

2 ounces goat cheese

Splash of vanilla extract

Pinch salt

**CHERUB TOMATO CONFIT**

1 pint cherry tomatoes

12 ounces water

8 ounces sugar

3 ounces glucose

Salt to taste

Pinch of black pepper

¼ ounce sherry vinegar

**ROASTED TOMATO SORBET**

16 ounces ripe tomatoes

6 ounces light corn syrup

6 ounces sugar

6 ounces water

1 ounce kosher salt

1 ounce sherry vinegar

**DEHYDRATED TOMATO SALT**

1 whole large tomato

1 ounce sea salt, preferably
    maldon salt

**TOMATO PAPER**

8 ounces tomato purée

4 ounces egg whites

4 ounces corn syrup

**SHERRY VINEGAR REDUCTION**

6 ounces sherry vinegar

2 ounces sugar

**PISTACHIO CRUMBLE**

1 pound Sicilian pistachios

2 ounces all-purpose flour

Kosher salt to taste

2 ounces sugar

2 ounces butter

**FOR THE GOAT CHEESE FONDANT:** Bloom gelatin in ice water for 5 minutes or until soft. Remove from water, squeeze out excess moisture and leave on a towel. In a medium sauce pot, heat cream and sugar to scalding point. Remove from heat. Add goat cheese, vanilla, salt, and bloomed gelatin and mix well, being careful not to incorporate too much air. Pour in plastic wrap–lined quarter sheet tray and refrigerate to set. If needed, freeze fondant to make cutting easier.

**FOR CHERUB TOMATO CONFIT:** Wash tomatoes and reserve. Combine water, sugar, and glucose in a medium sauce pot. Heat to a boil and cook to a syrupy consistency. Add salt, a pinch of ground black pepper, and vinegar. Mix well and pour hot syrup over tomatoes to begin to cook and candy them. Cover the container with plastic wrap to trap heat. Let cool to room temperature and refrigerate to store.

**FOR THE ROASTED TOMATO SORBET:** In a 400° F oven, roast the tomatoes until the skins begin to char and split off the flesh. In a blender, add the hot roasted tomatoes, corn syrup, and sugar and blend. Add the water and mix well. Add salt and sherry vinegar and cool over an ice bath. Strain the sorbet base through a fine mesh sieve. Spin the sorbet in ice cream machine according to manufacturer's instructions.

**FOR THE DEHYDRATED TOMATO SALT:** In a blender, purée the tomato and spread over an acetate sheet. Place in a dehydrator overnight, or in a gas oven with the pilot light on or in an electric oven set to 100° F. Peel the dried tomato off of the acetate and crumble with the sea salt. Reserve in airtight container for later use.

**FOR THE TOMATO PAPER:** Combine all ingredients in a blender. Spread the tomato mixture on a sheet of acetate and dehydrate overnight. Peel tomato paper off acetate and store in an airtight container.

**FOR THE SHERRY VINEGAR REDUCTION:** Place sherry vinegar and sugar in a small sauce pot and reduce by 4 times to achieve a syrup consistency. Remove from heat and reserve at room temperature.

**FOR THE PISTACHIO CRUMBLE:** Preheat oven to 350° F. To make pistachio flour, in a food processor, grind Sicilian pistachios to a fine consistency, but not paste-like. Remove from blender and measure out 4 ounces to use for crumble. In the same food processor, blend flour, salt, and sugar until the mixture is well combined. Cut butter into small cubes and pulse into the mixture until it is a sandy consistency. Add half of the pistachio flour back into the mixture and pulse until well combined. Mix remaining pistachio flour into the dough by hand, spread evenly on a sheet pan, and bake 10 to 12 minutes, or until edges are golden. Once crumble has cooled, break apart with hands and reserve at room temperature in an airtight container until needed.

**ASSEMBLY:** Place about 1 ounce of pistachio crumble centered on a square plate. Place a piece of goat cheese fondant on top of the crumble. Lay a quenelle of the roasted tomato sorbet next to the fondant. Place 3 confit cherub tomatoes around the dessert. Drizzle the sherry reduction around the crumble, next to the confit tomatoes. Finish the plate with a sprinkle of tomato salt, and place tomato paper next to the sorbet. Serve immediately.

# TOBACCO CREAM
## *CHOCOLATE SORBET, MAPLE BUDINO, HUCKLEBERRY, PECAN*

THIS WAS A PLAY ON CIGARETTES AND ALCOHOL. IT'S BASICALLY A SET CREAM, LIKE A PANNA COTTA, WITH INFUSED TOBACCO. WE DIP THE CREAM INTO A SCOTCH GEL THAT ADHERES TO IT. IT'S A REALLY STRANGE FLAVOR AT FIRST, BUT IT WORKS. WE COMPLEMENT IT WITH HUCKLEBERRY COULIS AND, OF COURSE, DARK CHOCOLATE.

**FOR THE TOBACCO CREAM:** Bloom the gelatin in ice water until soft and pliable, about 5 minutes, squeeze out excess water, and reserve. Heat the cream, salt, tobacco, and sugar, bringing the mixture just to the boiling point. Remove from heat and let infuse for 20 minutes. Pour the liquid through a sieve to remove the tobacco. While the mixture is still hot, add the gelatin and mix well to combine. Pour the cream in desired mold and set in the freezer for encapsulation.

**FOR THE SCOTCH GEL:** Heat the scotch and the alginate in a medium saucepan, then blend to incorporate. Let the gel sit overnight to release all air bubbles. Dip the set tobacco cream into the scotch gel and let sit for 1 minute. Remove from gel and a thin lining of scotch will encase the tobacco cream. Reserve for use.

**FOR THE MAPLE BUDINO:** Heat the half and half, vanilla, and maple syrup to the boiling point in a medium pan. In a large stainless bowl mix the egg, yolk, salt, sugar, and cornstarch. Mix well and slowly temper heated half and half with the egg mixture. Return to medium heat and continue to cook while constantly whisking. It should have a thick pudding-like consistency. Remove from heat and mix in butter. Cool over an ice bath and reserve.

**FOR THE CHOCOLATE SORBET:** Bring trimoline, salt, and water to a boil. Pour over chocolate and whisk to combine. Cool over ice bath. Prepare in ice cream machine according to manufacturer's directions.

**FOR THE CANDIED PECANS:** In a medium-size sauce pot, bring sugar and water to a boil. Add pecans and cook for 15 minutes over low heat. In a frying pan or skillet, heat up enough oil to submerge the cooked pecans. Fry pecans until crispy and toss in kosher salt.

**FOR THE HUCKLEBERRY COULIS:** Combine all ingredients in a small sauce pot and cook on medium heat until the huckleberries are falling apart and slow bubbles form in the mixture. Remove from heat and blend until well incorporated. Reserve ¼ of the coulis for the huckleberry paper.

**FOR THE HUCKLEBERRY PAPER:** Spread a thin sheet of reserved huckleberry coulis across an acetate sheet and dehydrate overnight in a dehydrator, or in a gas oven with the pilot light on or in an electric oven set to 100º F.

**ASSEMBLY:** On a rectangular plate, spread a large spoonful of maple budino to create a swoosh of the pudding. Place the encapsulated tobacco cream on top of the budino. Place a quenelle of chocolate sorbet next to the cream. Place dots of coulis across the plate. Finish with candied pecans and huckleberry paper. Serve immediately.

**TOBACCO CREAM**
2 sheets gelatin
Ice water
8 ounces heavy cream
1 pinch kosher salt
1 pinch high-quality tobacco
1 ounce sugar

**SCOTCH GEL**
25 ounces high-quality Islay Scotch
¼ ounce sodium alginate

**MAPLE BUDINO**
8 ounces half and half
⅛ ounce vanilla extract
1 ounce maple syrup
1 egg
1 egg yolk
Kosher salt
1½ ounces brown sugar
1 tablespoon cornstarch
1 ounce butter

**CHOCOLATE SORBET**
1 ounce trimoline
Kosher salt to taste
10 ounces water
6 ounces 66 percent cacao chocolate

**CANDIED PECAN**
6 ounces brown sugar
6 ounces water
4 ounces pecan halves
Frying oil
Kosher salt

**HUCKLEBERRY COULIS**
6 ounces huckleberry
2 ounces sugar
2 ounces water

**TOBACCO CREAM**

# GLOSSARY

**AGAR AGAR** TASTELESS DRIED SEAWEED THAT ACTS AS A SETTING AGENT OR GELATIN.
**AJI** HORSE MACKEREL.
**AMAEBI** RAW SWEET SHRIMP.
**ANAGO** SEA EEL. SOMETIMES CALLED CONGER EEL.
**AOYAGI** ROUND CLAM.
**AWABI** ABALONE.
**BLANCH** TO BRIEFLY PLUNGE FOOD INTO BOILING WATER AND THEN INTO COLD WATER TO STOP THE COOKING PROCESS.
**BONITO FLAKES** DRIED SMOKED SKIPJACK SHAVINGS.
**BOQUERONES** SPANISH WHITE ANCHOVIES.
**BOTTARGA** MEDITERRANEAN-STYLE CURED FISH ROE.
**BRUNOISE** 1/8-INCH PERFECT DICE.
**BURI** ADULT YELLOWTAIL.
**CALCIUM CHLORIDE / LACTATE** A NONSODIUM-BASED SALT USED TO ADD CALCIUM TO A LIQUID, WHICH SETS SODIUM ALGINATE–BASED LIQUID (I.E. FAUX CAVIARS, SPHERES, ENCAPSULATION).
**CARAGEENAN** SEAWEED-BASED PRODUCT USED AS A "GEL-IFIER" THAT CAN SUSTAIN HIGHER TEMPERATURES (I.E. HOT GELÉES).
**CARAMELIZE** TO HEAT FOOD TO THE POINT OF "BURNING" ITS NATURAL SUGARS OR TO "BURN" SUGAR TO FORM A CRISP SHELL.
**CARDAMOM** COMES FROM THE GINGER FAMILY AND IS THE THIRD MOST EXPENSIVE SPICE IN THE WORLD, FOLLOWING SAFFRON AND VANILLA.
**CHIFFONADE** THIN STRIPS OR SHREDS OF VEGETABLES.
**CHUTNEY** A SWEET AND SPICY CONDIMENT CONTAINING FRUIT, VINEGAR, SUGAR, AND SPICES. CAN BE SMOOTH OR CHUNKY.
**CHUTORO** MARBLED TUNA BELLY.
**CITRIC ACID** A STRONG, TART WHITE POWDER EXTRACTED FROM JUICE OF CITRUS AND OTHER ACIDIC FRUITS.
**CLAM** BIVALVE MOLLUSK. CAN BE HARD- OR SOFT-SHELLED AND USUALLY HAS A FIRMER TEXTURE.

**CLARIFY** TO CLEAR A CLOUDY LIQUID BY REMOVING SEDIMENT.
**CONCASSÉ** COARSELY CHOPPED OR GROUND MIXTURE.
**CONFIT** TO SALT FOOD AND SLOWLY COOK IT IN ITS OWN JUICES OR FAT.
**CONSOMMÉ** CLARIFIED MEAT OR FISH BROTH.
**COULIS** THICK PURÉE OR SAUCE.
**CURE** TO TREAT FOOD IN ORDER TO PRESERVE IT.
**DAIKON** A MILD-FLAVORED JAPANESE GIANT WHITE RADISH.
**DANGO** THE RICE ON WHICH THE NETA SETS IN A NIGIRI PIECE, I.E. THE RICE UNDER THE FISH.
**DASHI** TRADITIONAL JAPANESE STOCK FROM KOMBU (KELP) AND KATSUOBUSHI (LITERALLY "JACKFISH SHAVINGS"). DASHI FORMS THE BASE FOR MISO SOUPS, CLEAR BROTH SOUPS, JAPANESE NOODLE BROTHS, AND MANY JAPANESE SIMMER-ING LIQUIDS. PURE DASHI IS CONSIDERED TO HAVE UMAMI, THE FIFTH FLAVOR.
**DICE** TINY CUBES, USUALLY 1 TO 1/4 INCH.
**EBI** BLACK TIGER SHRIMP FROM THAILAND OR VIETNAM.
**EMULSION** SLOW ADDITION OF ONE LIQUID TO ANOTHER WHILE RAPIDLY MIXING, USED TO MIX LIQUIDS THAT NORMALLY DO NOT BLEND, SUCH AS OIL AND WATER.
**FISH CARAMEL** SWEETENED FISH SAUCE REDUCTION.
**FIVE-SPICE BLEND** CONSISTS OF PEPPERCORN, CORIANDER, CLOVE, CINNAMON, AND STAR ANISE.
**FURIKAKE** A SHAKEN SEA-SONING TO ACCOMPANY RICE OR TOFU. OURS INCLUDES STRIPS OF NORI, DRIED EGG, SESAME SEEDS, SALT, AND MONOSODIUM GLUTAMATE (FOR FLAVOR).
**GASTRIQUE** A SYRUPY REDUC-TION OF CARAMELIZED SUGAR AND VINEGAR.
**GELÉE** FRENCH WORD FOR JELLY, MOST OFTEN MADE WITH GELATIN.
**GELLAN** AN AEROBIC BACTE-RIA-BASED SUBSTANCE USED AS A STABILIZER, EMULSIFIER,

AND THICKENER THAT CAN SUSTAIN HIGHER TEMPERATURES.
**GOMA** SESAME SEED.
**GRANITÉ** SLOWLY FROZEN, FLAVORED ICE CRYSTALS.
**GRILL** TO PREPARE FOOD ON A GRATE OVER HOT COALS OR OTHER HEAT SOURCE.
**HAMACHI** YELLOWTAIL JACK-FISH; NOT TO BE CONFUSED WITH YELLOWFIN TUNA.
**HIRAME** FLOUNDER. A FLAT WHITEFISH THAT IS A BOTTOM-FEEDER AND LIES BENEATH THE SAND ON THE OCEAN FLOOR AND CAN BE CLASSIFIED AS A FLUKE. YOU CAN DISTIN-GUISH THIS PIECE OF SUSHI FROM THE OTHER WHITEFISH BY ITS LUMINESCENCE.
**HOTATE** SCALLOPS. FROM THE NORTH ATLANTIC.
**IKA** SQUID.
**IKURA** SALMON ROE. SALTY; CONTRASTS NICELY WITH UNI, OR SEA URCHIN.
**IMMERSION CIRCULATOR** LAB / KITCHEN TOOL THAT HOLDS LIQUID AT A SPECIFIC, EXACT TEMPERATURE, USED MOST FREQUENTLY FOR EXTENDED LOW TEMPERATURE COOKING.
**INFUSION** FLAVOR EXTRACTED FROM AN ITEM BY STEEPING IN A LIQUID.
**JULIENNE** THIN, MATCHSTICK-SIZED CUTS.
**KABOCHA** A WINTER SQUASH WITH GREEN SKIN THAT HAS TASTE AND TEXTURE SIMILAR TO BUTTERNUT SQUASH, AKA JAPANESE PUMPKIN.
**KAFFIR LIME LEAVES** DARK LEAVES OF SMALL, PEAR-SHAPED CITRUS WITH INTENSE FRA-GRANCE.
**KAIWARE** DAIKON RADISH SPROUTS.
**KAJIKI** SWORDFISH.
**KANI KAMA** IMITATION CRAB.
**KANPACHI** VERY YOUNG YELLOWTAIL.
**KARASHI** TRADITIONALLY, A DRY MUSTARD PASTE THAT IS VERY SPICY.
**KATSUO** BONITO.
**KEGANI** LITERALLY TRANS-LATED TO MEAN HAIRY CRAB.
**KEWPIE MAYONNAISE** MOST POPULAR MAYONNAISE IN

JAPAN. NOT TOO SWEET.
**KIKURAGE** DRIED MUSH-ROOM-TYPE FUNGUS COM-MONLY USED IN ASIAN COOKING. MAY BE FOUND AT MOST ASIAN MARKETS.
**KIMCHEE** IS A TRADITIONAL KOREAN DISH, MADE OF VEGETABLES WITH VARIED SEASONINGS. UCHI USES A VARIATION OF A KIMCHEE BASE TO SEASON VEGETABLES AND SOME FRUITS SUCH AS APPLES AND PEACHES.
**KRAB** FAKE CRAB MADE FROM POLLOCK.
**MAGURO / AKAMI** MOST COMMON PART OF THE TUNA FAMILY, GENERALLY BLUEFIN. IT USUALLY HAS A DEEP RED COLOR AND A FIRMER TEXTURE THAN TORO. THE TERM HON-MAGURO MAY BE USED ONLY TO DESCRIBE BLUEFIN TUNA, WHICH IS CONSIDERED BY THE JAPANESE TO BE THE ONLY REAL TUNA. THE TERMS AKAMI AND MAGURO MAY BE USED INTERCHANGEABLY; AKAMI MEANS "RED MEAT." YELLOW-FIN TENDS TO BE INFERIOR SINCE IT IS A SURFACE LEVEL FISH. IT HAS LESS FAT BECAUSE OF WARMER WATER TEMPERA-TURES WHERE IT DWELLS, AND SO YOU CANNOT GET TORO FROM YELLOWFIN. THERE ARE SEVERAL DIFFERENT GRADES OF TORO THAT UCHI MAY SERVE:
*TORO:* FATTY TUNA.
*CHU TORO:* MEDIUM FAT PART OF THE BELLY. IT IS SOFTER AND HAS MORE FLAVOR THAN AKAMI BUT IS NOT AS OVER-WHELMING AS O TORO.
*KAMA TORO:* FATTY TUNA TAKEN FROM THE CHEEK.
*O TORO:* CONSIDERED THE FINEST CUT. THE MOST EXPENSIVE PART OF THE TUNA BECAUSE ONLY A SMALL PIECE CAN BE CUT FROM THE TUNA. A LITTLE TOO FATTY FOR MOST AMERICAN PALATES.
*SUPER TORO:* DENOTES OUR YOUNG, FARM-RAISED BLUEFIN TUNA.
**MADAI** JAPANESE RED SEA BREAM. VERY FRESH WHITE-FISH WITH A CLEAN, RESILIENT TEXTURE. YOU CAN DISTINGUISH

THIS PIECE OF SUSHI FROM THE OTHER WHITEFISH BY ITS WHITE HUE.
**MASAGO** SMELT ROE. SWEETER THAN TOBIKO AND MORE OPAQUE IN APPEARANCE.
**MASU** TROUT.
**MATAGAI** RAZOR CLAM.
**MATSUTAKE** DARK BROWN JAPANESE WILD MUSHROOM WITH A DENSE, MEATY TEXTURE AND NUTTY, FRAGRANT FLAVOR.
**MICRO-BRUNOISE** 1/16-INCH PERFECT DICE.
**MIRIN** THICK, SWEET RICE WINE.
**MIRUGAI** GEODUCK CLAM.
**MISO** FERMENTED SOYBEAN PASTE OFTEN USED AS A BASE IN SOUPS AND SAUCES.
**MONOGLYCERIDE** A CHEMICAL AGENT ADDED TO FAT THAT WILL ALLOW EMULSIFICATION WITH OTHER PRODUCTS (I.E. OIL AND WATER).
**MUSSEL** BIVALVE MOLLUSK WITH LONG, THIN SHELLS WITH TOUGHER, MEATY TEXTURE.
**MYOGA** VARIEGATED JAPANESE GINGER. TASTES LIKE A CROSS BETWEEN A GARLIC/SHALLOT AND TRADITIONAL GINGER.
**NEGI** GREEN ONIONS.
**NETA** ANYTHING THAT SITS ON TOP OF DANGO, I.E. THE FISH THAT SITS ON TOP OF THE RICE POD IN NIGIRI SUSHI.
**NIGIRI** REFERS TO STYLE OF SUSHI WHERE FISH IS PLACED ATOP VINEGARED RICE BALLS. NOT TO BE CONFUSED WITH NIGORI, A TYPE OF UNFILTERED SAKE.
**NORI** SEAWEED PAPER.
**ONIGIRI** HANDMADE RICE BALL.
**O TORO** FATTY PORTION OF TUNA BELLY.
**OYSTER** BIVALVE MOLLUSK WITH A THICK, BUMPY SHELL THAT IS TYPICALLY SERVED RAW. FLAVORS RANGE FROM MILD TO BRINY AND TEXTURES RANGE FROM TENDER TO FIRM.
**PANKO** COARSE BREAD CRUMBS USED IN JAPANESE COOKING FOR CRUNCHY TEXTURE.
**PATTYPAN SQUASH** ROUND, FLAT SUMMER SQUASH, AKA SUMMER SQUASH.
**PERIWINKLE** SMALL SEA SNAILS.

UCHI, THE COOKBOOK

254

**PIPERADE** A MIXTURE OF TO-MATOES AND SWEET PEPPERS COOKED IN OLIVE OIL.

**PONZU** SOY, RED WINE VIN-EGAR, AND CITRUS JUICES.

**PRESSURE-COOK** TO COOK FOOD IN A TEMPERATURE- AND PRESSURE-CONTROLLED POT AT A VERY HIGH TEMPERATURE.

**PURÉE** ANY FOOD THAT IS FINELY MASHED TO A SMOOTH, THICK CONSISTENCY.

**QUENELLE** THE OVAL-SHAPED SCOOP IN WHICH DESSERT SORBETS AT UCHI ARE SERVED.

**REDUCTION** BOILING A LIQUID RAPIDLY UNTIL VOLUME IS REDUCED BY EVAPORATION, CAUSING FLAVORS TO INTENSIFY AND CONSISTENCY TO THICKEN.

**RENDER** MELT ANIMAL FAT OVER LOW HEAT TO SEPARATE IT FROM CONNECTIVE TISSUE

**SABA** NORWEGIAN MACKEREL. SALTED AND COOKED IN VIN-EGAR (CURED).

**SAKANA** FISH (THE SHUN NO SAKANA ON THE SPECIALS PAGE REFERS TO THE "FISH OF THE DAY").

**SAKE** ATLANTIC SALMON; ALL FARM-RAISED THAT IS PINK IN COLOR AND VERY FATTY. THE BREED IS ATLANTIC BUT IT IS NOT NECESSARILY FROM THE ATLANTIC.

**SAKE LEES** LEES COMES FROM SAKE DREGS (SEDIMENT), WHICH IS THE SOLID MATTER LEFT OVER FROM THE MILLING OF RICE FOR WINE PRODUCTION.

**SAN BAI ZU** VINEGAR, SOY, DASHI, AND SUGAR.

**SANMA** SAURY.

**SASAMI** CHICKEN.

**SASHIMI** RAW FISH (WITHOUT RICE).

**SATSUMAIMO** JAPANESE MOUNTAIN POTATO, COMPA-RABLE TO A SWEET POTATO.

**SAUTÉ** TO COOK FOOD QUICKLY IN A SMALL AMOUNT OF OIL IN A SKILLET OR PAN.

**SAWARA** SPANISH MACKEREL.

**SAYORI** HALF BEAK FISH IMPORTED FROM JAPAN.

**SCALE** TO REMOVE SCALES FROM A FISH.

**SEAR** TO BROWN MEAT BY SUBJECTING IT VERY HIGH

HEAT, IN A SKILLET, UNDER A BROILER, OR IN AN OVEN TO SEAL IN JUICES.

**SHIMA-AJI** STRIPED JACK.

**SHIO** SALT.

**SHIRO SAKE** WHITE SALMON.

**SHIROMI** SEASONAL "WHITE MEAT" FISH.

**SHISO** JAPANESE MINT LEAF ALSO KNOWN AS OOBA.

**SHOYU** SOY SAUCE.

**SIMPLE SYRUP** A MIX OF EQUAL PARTS DISSOLVED SUGAR AND WATER.

**SODIUM ALGINATE** AN ALGAE-BASED GUM USED AS A THICKENER; IT IS COMBINED WITH CALCIUM LACTATE TO CREATE SPHERES SURROUNDED BY A THIN JELLY MEMBRANE.

**SOIL / CRUMBLE** A BAKED MIXTURE OF SUGAR AND FLOUR, USUALLY CONTAINING SPICES, NUTS, ETC. CRUMBLED AFTER COOLING TO RESEMBLE DIRT IN APPEARANCE AND TEXTURE.

**SORBET** A SMOOTH-TEXTURED FLAVORED ICE THAT NEVER CONTAINS MILK. MAY BE SAVORY OR SWEET.

**SOUS VIDE** FRENCH WORD FOR "UNDER VACUUM"—TO COOK PRODUCTS IN AIRTIGHT BAGS FOR EXTENDED PERIODS OF TIME AT A CONSTANT, SPECIFIC TEMPERATURE, MOST OFTEN USING A THERMAL CIRCULATOR.

**SOY LECITHIN** SOYBEAN-BASED PRODUCT USED TO CRE-ATE FOAM, AIR, ESPUMA, ETC.

**SPICE TRIO** CONSISTS OF TOGARASHI (SEVEN-SPICE COMBINATION: CHILE PEPPER, ORANGE PEEL, BLACK SESAME SEEDS, NORI, WHITE SESAME, SANSHO PEPPER, GINGER), AWASE SHIO (MIXTURE OF KOSHER SALT AND WHITE PEP-PER) AND A PEPPER BLEND.

**SPICY AIOLI** CONSISTS OF KEWPIE MAYONNAISE, MOMIJI PEPPER SAUCE, MASAGO, GREEN ONIONS, AND SESAME OIL.

**SQUID INK SU MISO** A DARK, SWEET SAUCE MADE FROM VINEGAR, MISO, AND SQUID INK. THE SWEETNESS COMES FROM THE VINEGAR AND MISO COMBINATION. A VERY SMALL

AMOUNT OF SQUID INK IS USED TO COLOR THE SAUCE.

**SRIRACHA** SUN-DRIED ASIAN RED CHILE SAUCE.

**STABILIZER** ADDITIVES USED TO MAINTAIN EMULSIONS OR PREVENT DEGENERATION IN FOOD.

**STEAM** TO COOK FOOD OVER, NOT SUBMERGED IN, BOILING OR SIMMERING WATER IN A COVERED PAN.

**SUCROESTER** A SUGAR-BASED CHEMICAL AGENT ADDED TO WATER TO EMULSIFY INTO A FATTY MEDIUM (I.E. OIL AND WATER).

**SUSHI** COLD RICE DRESSED WITH VINEGAR, FORMED INTO ANY VARIOUS SHAPES, AND GARNISHED ESPECIALLY WITH BITS OF RAW SEAFOOD OR VEGETABLES. THE JAPANESE TRANSLATION MEANS "VIN-EGAR" (SU) "RICE" (SHI).

**SUZUKI** STRIPED SEA BASS. A SMALL, FRESH WHITEFISH THAT DEGENERATES IMMEDI-ATELY. YOU CAN DISTINGUISH THIS PIECE OF SUSHI FROM THE OTHER WHITEFISH BY ITS TRANSLUCENT, PINK HUE.

**TAI** SEA BREAM.

**TAIRAGAI** JAPANESE PEN SHELL CLAM.

**TAMAGO** EGG.

**TAMARI** TAMARI IS THE NAME FOR A TYPE OF VERY DARK SOY. UCHI TYPICALLY MIXES THIS WITH WHITE SOY, WHICH HAS DASHI ADDED TO ADD FLAVOR AND DEPTH.

**TANIN BUNE** HALF IKURA, HALF UNI, GUNKAN STYLE.

**TARABA** SNOW CRAB.

**TARE** CLASSIC JAPANESE SAUCE CONSISTING OF SOY, HONEY, SAKE, MIRIN, GINGER, GARLIC, SCALLIONS, AND CHILE.

**TATAKI** SEARED OCTOPUS.

**TEMAKI** HANDROLL.

**TEN-TSUYU** SAUCE WITH SOY AND MIRIN. WIDELY USED AS TEMPURA SAUCE AND ALSO KNOWN AS SOY-DASHI BROTH.

**TERRINE** A SEASONED MIX-TURE OF LIKE ITEMS, MOLDED INTO A TERRINE SHAPE.

**TOBIKO** FLYING FISH ROE. AVAILABLE IN ORANGE AND GOLDEN. THE GOLDEN IS MORE

RESILIENT AND THREE TIMES AS EXPENSIVE. THE ORANGE IS TRANSLUCENT COMPARED TO MASAGO.

**TOGARASHI** SEVEN-SPICE COMBINATION: CHILE PEPPER, ORANGE PEEL, BLACK SESAME SEEDS, NORI, WHITE SESAME, SANSHO PEPPER, GINGER.

**TORCHON** A SEASONED MIXTURE OF LIKE ITEMS, ROLLED INTO LOG SHAPE WITH THE AID OF A KITCHEN TOWEL.

**TRANSGLUTAMINASE** AKA MEAT GLUE—ENZYMES THAT PRODUCE INSOLUBLE PROTEIN POLYMERS USED FOR TER-RINES, ETC.

**TSUBUGAI** SEA SNAIL.

**TUILE/GLASS/PAPER** A THIN, CRISP "COOKIE" MADE FROM NUTS, CITRUS, SPICES, ETC.

**UNAGI** PRECOOKED AND SMOKED FRESHWATER EEL FROM KOREA.

**UNI** SEA URCHIN. THE EDIBLE PART OF UNI IS THE ASEXUAL REPRODUCTIVE ORGAN; HENCE IT IS CONSIDERED AN APH-RODISIAC IN JAPAN. UNI CAN COME FROM VARIOUS PLACES AND THE TASTE WILL DIFFER ACCORDINGLY.

**UMAMI** THE FIFTH TASTE, AKA THE "SAVORY" SENSE OF FLAVOR.

**UME** PICKLED JAPANESE PLUM.

**VACUUM-MARINATE** TECHNIQUE TO INFUSE FLAVOR INTO MEAT QUICKLY BY VACUUM SEALING.

**VACUUM-SEAL** TO SEAL AN ITEM IN A WAY THAT REMOVES AIR. THIS PROTECTS THE FOOD AND SLOWS THE DECOMPOSI-TION PROCESS.

**WAGYU BEEF** AMERICAN STOCK OF KOBE BEEF. WAGYU IS THE BREED OF THE COW, SO KOBE IS A WAGYU COW RAISED IN KOBE, JAPAN. SIMILAR TO HOW CHAMPAGNE IS A SPARKLING WINE FROM CHAM-PAGNE, FRANCE, OR THE DIF-FERENCE BETWEEN CHIANTI AND SANGIOVESE. THEREFORE UCHI "KOBE" IS A WAGYU COW FROM THE U.S. THE MEAT IS ORGANIC, ALL NATURAL, AND GRASS FED.

**WASABI** JAPANESE HORSE-RADISH. FRESH COMES FROM

THE ROOT VEGETABLE AND HAS AN IMMEDIATE BURN THAT DIS-SIPATES CLEAN AND QUICKLY. MOST COMMONLY PRODUCED IN PASTE AND POWDER FORMS, BLENDED WITH WATER AND SERVED AS A CONDIMENT.

**WHELK** LARGE MARINE SNAIL THAT IS SLIGHTLY TOUGH BUT FLAVORFUL.

**XANTHAM GUM** A THICKENER PRODUCED FROM FERMENTED CORN SUGAR.

**YAMAIMO** JAPANESE POTATO, PURPLE OR WHITE.

**YUCCA** A SWEET ROOT VEG-ETABLE, MUCH LIKE A POTATO OR TARO ROOT.

**YUKARI** DRIED RED SHISO, OR BEEFSTEAK PLANT. FLAVOR IS SIMILAR TO THAT OF A SMOKED TOMATO OR SMOKED TEA.

**YUZU** SOUR JAPANESE CITRUS PRIMARILY USED FOR THE RIND, FLAVOR SIMILAR TO LEMON AND LIME.

**YUZU KOSHO** A PASTE MADE AT UCHI FROM LIME ZEST, THAI CHILE, GARLIC, AND SALT. HOWEVER, THAT IS NOT HOW IT IS TRADITIONALLY MADE IN JAPAN.

# INDEX

# INDEX

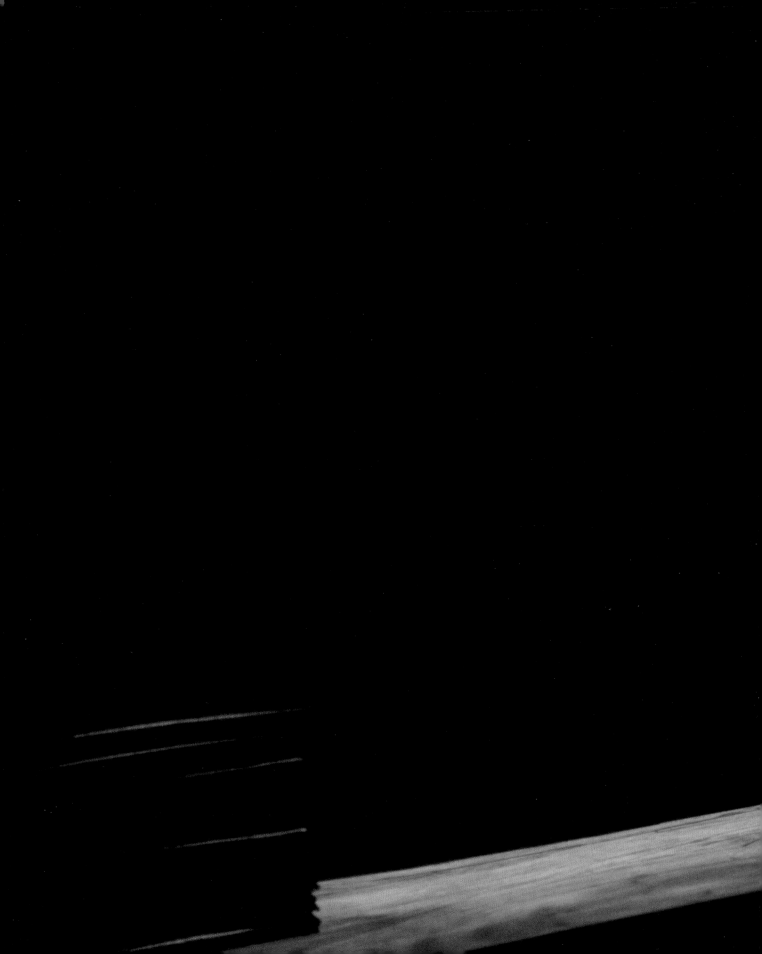

# ABOUT THE AUTHORS

**JESSICA DUPUY**

Jessica Dupuy is a freelance writer who has written for *National Geographic Traveler, Texas Monthly, Texas Highways,* and *Fodor's Travel Publications.* Dupuy's favorite writing pursuits are about the things she loves most in life: food, travel, and the outdoors. Dupuy received a bachelor's degree from Trinity University and a master's degree in Journalism from Northwestern University's Medill School of Journalism. She lives in Austin with her husband, Myers, her son, Gus, and two Duck Tolling retrievers, Finn and Ginger. She enjoys cooking, traveling, triathlons, and fly-fishing.

**TYSON COLE**

Tyson Cole, 40, is a passionate student of the Japanese tradition. Cole became fascinated with sushi in his early twenties while working at an Austin Japanese restaurant. He dedicated himself to learning every aspect of the cuisine. Demonstrating skill and dexterity with the knife, he quickly worked his way onto the sushi line at Austin's top sushi restaurant, Musashino, where he completed an intensive traditional apprenticeship under owner Takehiko Fuse. Fuse challenged him to learn the Japanese language, which helped Cole learn more about the cuisine. He later trained at Bond Street, one of the busiest sushi restaurants in New York City. In his last year at Musashino, Cole began experimenting with new ideas about flavors, influences, and ingredients, running the restaurant in Fuse's absence.

In May 2003 Uchi opened, with Cole as Executive Chef and co-owner. He continues his path of study and experimentation at Uchi, developing unprecedented multicultural combinations using his impeccable knowledge of technique. Cole's gift of marrying global ingredients and flavors with traditional Japanese flavors quickly garnered him local as well as national attention, and Uchi became one of the top fine dining restaurants in Austin. The accolades continued when he was awarded a coveted spot on *Food & Wine Magazine*'s Best New Chefs of 2005 list. Cole opened his second restaurant in Austin, Uchiko, in July 2010.

tyson cole
executive chef

uchi

就

This book is dedicated to those who have helped me along the way. From friends, family, my sushi sensei, and fellow Japanese chefs to those who insulted my efforts and said I couldn't do it. From all of you, I've learned, I've grown, and for that I'm grateful.

Becoming a sushi chef happened in a number of stages for me. It started with a part-time dishwashing job at a Japanese restaurant, where I fell in love with the Japanese culture and food. A culture based on respect for each other and the food we eat? Fantastic! My eyes were aglow with the possibilities; it was a brand new world of food and life, and I couldn't get enough. I wanted to soak in everything about it. To taste it. To eat it. To create it. Making sushi was what I was born to do.

That first job began years of headstrong work to become a sushi chef. Many times it seemed improbable, almost impossible. I got fired. I was insulted. There were people who refused to let me make their sushi just because I was white. At one point, I even had to make sushi in the kitchen, where no one could see me. But every challenge fed my passion even more. I wouldn't be denied my chance. I worked harder and more diligently for this career than for anything I had ever done in my life.

Over the years, I became good at it. Really good at it. I had mastered all the components required to become a great sushi chef: dexterity, speed, efficiency, eye-hand coordination (the result of playing sports and countless video games while growing up), multi-tasking, speaking multiple languages, leading, and creating—all while standing in front of a bar and a restaurant full of hungry customers waiting for me to piece out a full meal, bite by bite! Every day, regular customers would come back to me, asking me, "Make me something I've never had." They'd say, "Come up with something you've never made before!"

Like an impromptu performer, I was forced by those spontaneous requests over the years to improve. To experiment. To shine. Sushi is the greatest delicacy in the world to me, and I have become a craftsman. With a knife. A bandanna. A wooden board. And raw fish.

TYSON COLE